THE SILVER LINING

THE SILVER LINING

THE INTERSECTION OF SEXUAL ASSAULT AND ANXIETY THROUGH THE WORLD OF GYMNASTICS

SERENA PERGOLA

All proceeds will be donated to the Athlete Assistance Fund

NEW DEGREE PRESS

THE SILVER LINING

The Intersection of Sexual Assault and Anxiety

Through the World of Gymnastics

ISBN   978-1-64137-359-3 *Paperback*

          978-1-64137-698-3 *Ebook*

To my mom, Lisa Pergola, for always believing in me even when I found it too hard to believe in myself and for being my guiding light...

To Dani Messineo for supporting me through some of the darkest battles and helping me find my own light...

To Jen Webb for guiding me both in faith and in healing...

And to Olivia Velarde for empowering me to share my story and letting my voice be heard and for helping edit this book and shape it into what you will read here today.

CONTENTS

Change is possible if we all band together and BELIEVE in one another. No survivor should ever go unheard. Every voice is important and worthy of being heard. Speak your truth. No one should ever have to feel embarrassed that #MeToo applies to me too.

BACKGROUND

———

This is a deep dive into the love and loss in the sport of gymnastics. I explore how the culture influenced my experiences inside and outside of the gym's walls. This journey will stretch far beyond just the sport and welcome you into the inner workings of my life with the hope that I can empower you to find your silver lining, just like I have. Life is a marathon, let's run it side by side.

Trigger Warning: While there is no explicit content about sexual assault, I do want to warn those of you who this might be a sensitive subject for that there are allusions to these experiences. Avoid chapters 6, 9, and 10 if you wish to omit the content that discusses this topic. Additionally, I am happy to make myself a resource for anyone who is seeking support.

INTRODUCTION

EMBRACING YOUR SILVER LINING

I must zone back in, but the pain was all-encompassing. I will not be the problem. I will finish this meet.

Nothing short of being knocked out cold can stop a gymnast when they are in the competition mindset. Resilience to the point of pure stubbornness is demonstrated on the competition floor more often than not. Yet, gymnasts are always coming back for more.

Healthy passion or painful addiction? That interpretation is up to you.

* * *

Gymnastics is known as one of the most high-risk sports in the National Collegiate Athletic Association (NCAA), as extreme stresses may occur during characteristic maneuvers of the sport.[1]

Research indicates that female athletes in judged sports have a thirteen percent prevalence of eating disorders, compared to just three percent in the general population.[2]

At least 368 gymnasts have accused coaches, gym owners, and other adults in the sport with sexual misconduct over the last twenty years. That's one every twenty days. Experts say the actual number is likely much higher. That's because many victims—research indicates it could be as high as sixty-five to eighty percent—never report sexual abuse.[3]

The question then becomes, how do we salvage the passionate love developed for the sport and also eliminate the horrendous pain caused from the sport?

* * *

1   Westermann, R., Giblin, M., Vaske, A., Grosso, K. and Wolf, B. *Evaluation of Men's and Women's Gymnastics Injuries.* National Center for Biotechnology Information. (2015).

2   Ekern, J. "Risks of Eating Disorders for Athletes & Successful Recovery." *Eating Disorder Hope.* (2011).

3   Evans, T., Alesia, M. and Kwiatkowski, M. "Indystar's Investigation on Sexual Abuse in Gymnastics: What We Know," *Indystar.Com.* (2016).

There I was, standing in the doorway of the University of Michigan gymnastics practice facility.

As a freshman, I was there as a last-ditch effort to hold onto my infatuating love. Instead, what I was faced with was an identity-crushing loss. I stood staring into a gym filled with equipment that I would never practice on, and that was a hard fact for me to swallow. I walked away and did not turn back again, until my senior year when I found myself in that very same doorway. I rediscovered the passion I had been longing to get back.

I didn't want to dislike the sport, but I needed to place blame somewhere and it was easier to place it on the inanimate sport of gymnastics that had abandoned me rather than on the very animate individuals who had caused all the trauma in my life.

A simple Google search of "Why gymnastics is bad" produces headlines such as "The Dangerous Effects of Gymnastics for Developing Children," "Competitive Gymnastics is Broken," "The Darker Side of Competitive Gymnastics for Kids," and "The Heartbreaking Dark Side of Women's Gymnastics."

And, of course, the infamous Larry Nassar trial isn't exactly good press for the sport.

But there is so much more to the story than just the horrific things that Nassar did. Take, for instance, all of the following inspiring quotes that women stated while testifying:

"Life's handed me lemons, and you'd best believe that I am well prepared to make lemonade."—Hannah Morrow, gymnast

"Larry, I hope you … and all others realize you've pissed off the wrong army of women."—Lindsey Lemke, Michigan State student and gymnast

"The road to healing looks steep from where I am standing now, but I am a warrior."—Jennifer Rood-Bedford, MSU student and volleyball player

"You made a critical mistake. You underestimated the mind, power, and will of your victims, these accomplished athletes."—Kaylee Lorincz, gymnast

"All these brave women have power, and we will use our voices to make sure you get what you deserve: A life of suffering spent replaying the words delivered by this powerful army of survivors."—Aly Raisman, Olympic gymnast

This leaves me with one question, why has a sport that I love so much, that all gymnasts love so much, also led to so much pain and suffering for me and for others?

Most importantly, how can we reconcile this pain with a sport and culture of passion and love?

* * *

It is clear, the gymnastics world is experiencing deep-rooted conflict as of late.

A former federal prosecutor's review found that "it (gymnastics) needed a complete culture change."[4]

There is a tension between believing it is all positive or it is all negative. The reality, however, is somewhere in between. The real problem, as it stands, is the culture.

It has nothing to do with the sport in its purest form, but rather it has everything to do with the culture that surrounds the sport and infiltrates it with corruption and negativity. This culture does not have to be the end all be all. In fact, this is the perfect time to begin to explore the positives of the sport that have since been overshadowed by the negatives.

This is a collection of stories, of both loss and hurt, mostly from me, but also from some of those around me. This journey of telling my story has helped me to uncover that I am

---

4   Evans, T. "Child Advocate, Former Prosecutor Join USA Gymnastics in Move to Better Protect Athletes." *Indystar.Com.* (2017).

not alone. From people as high profile as Aly Raisman to those who have just come into my life, like an anonymous Nassar survivor, and finally to those much closer to home, like my life-long friend Brooke, I have surrounded myself with people who can offer me support and understanding. Brooke will discuss the struggles of body image anxiety, the anonymous Nassar survivor will explore the concept of being a warrior, and finally I will mirror my experiences with Aly Raisman's to demonstrate how someone both high profile and completely under the radar can suffer in the same ways.

* * *

You'll hear stories including:

- The Sad Truth That All I'll Ever Be Is Just a Gymnast

- You Don't Always Have to Fit in

- There Is Plenty of Light Still Left to Spread

- The Jagged Path of Coping and Healing in the Wide World of Therapy

- A Letter From My Mom: Open Your Hearts... and Your Ears

- In a World Where You Can Be Anything, Be Kind

These are stories of intoxicating (and maybe toxic at times) love, heart-wrenching loss, and falling in passionate love again. But this isn't a traditional love story.

In fact, this story only involves one person: myself, and, of course, the sport of gymnastics. The funny thing about my heart-wrenching loss and my passionate love is that they both happened in the very same spot.

* * *

Silver Lining.

noun

: a consoling or hopeful prospect[5]

I felt compelled to write this because I have this passion inside of me to empower others to find their silver lining, just as I have been empowered to find my own. I want to spread this sense of community and confidence to those who feel just as alone and worthless as I did on my darkest day. I not only look backward and describe the trauma and the pain, but I look deeper and explore the therapy process and the support systems, and, finally, I look forward at how you can leverage these things to make yourself stronger than ever before. I feel I am in a position to be able to share my

---

5   Definition of Silver lining. *Merriam-Webster.Com.* (2019).

story with you, the raw and honest truths of it, and what the process of fighting, coping, and healing looks like.

This is a story of lessons from tragedy, loss, and falling back in love with both myself and the sport of gymnastics.

I want to share this journey with anyone and everyone who is willing to open themselves up to letting me in. I specifically want to connect with those young gymnasts, former gymnasts, and parents of gymnasts who share my passion for the invaluable sport of gymnastics.

And with that being said, I welcome you to my most intimate stories.

THE UNTOUCHABLE SUBJECT

—

I was afraid
Ashamed
I refused to admit
#MeToo

"Just get over it already"
"Out of sight, out of mind"
"Don't be dramatic"
"You're lying"

I have been told
Not to talk about it:
The Untouchable Subject.

Complete and utter denial
That what I was experiencing
Was more than just stress
I had undergone legitimate trauma.

Anxiety
A figure of my imagination.
Then, it wasn't.

Drowning at the bottom of the ocean,
Screaming for help;
No one could hear me.

A large boulder tied to my ankles,
Restraining my release;
I could not swim to the top.
Fetal position,
Shaking vigorously,
Struggling for what felt like my last breath.

Manufactured smile,
Painted on for the outside world.
Don't let them know,
I was crumbling inside.
Stifling my emotions,
My lungs clenching one another for support.

I was helpless.
I was defeated.
I was convinced this would never end.

Healing is a process
A long, winding road
There is no light at the end of the tunnel
To tell you you're doing it "right."

Sitting across from my therapist:
"What if she judges **me too**?"
"What if she thinks I'm dramatic?"
"What if she thinks I'm lying?"

Button downs for the workplace,
Miniskirts for the nightclub,
Low cut shirts for your first date,
Sweaters for your family function.

My clothes don't give consent,
I do.

The past is just that,
It's in the past.
Dwelling on the negative,
Prolongs the positive.

Stand up,
Speak up.
Tell your story.
Be empowered.

A new day grants
A new chance
At a new beginning.

There are ups,
There are downs,
But you would never know the difference,
If you didn't experience them both.

I am a survivor.
I am coping.
I am healing.

It's okay,
That **#MeToo**
Applies to **me too**.

PART ONE

LOOKING BACKWARD

CHAPTER 1

HOW MY FIRST LOVE BECAME MY UNDYING ADDICTION

―――

I was three when I first stepped onto a gymnastics mat. It was a birthday party at the local gym, Phoenix Gymnastics, and I had never been to a gymnastics party before. One walk across the beam, ten swings on the bars, twenty bounces down the tumble track, thirty tumblesalts later and I couldn't get enough of the feeling it was inciting within me. Mind you, I was three years old and I had no idea what that feeling was at the time. I can now confirm, a little less than twenty years later, that the feeling was in fact love.

* * *

The addiction to gymnastics from a young age is not uncommon. In fact, young Romanians were so obsessed with the sport that they were willing to lie just to get out onto the Olympic floor.

"Teenage Romanian girls were ordered to lie about their ages to be allowed to compete in gymnastics competitions including the Olympics, a Romanian coach has admitted. The head of the Romanian Gymnastics Federation, Nicolae Vieru, said the practice was widespread during the last decade."[6]

* * *

My love affair with gymnastics was innocent at first. I joined the recreational gymnastics program and went to a one-hour class once a week in a gym that smelled like a mix of sweat and perfume. The radio boomed with songs such as "Stronger," by Kanye West, "Rehab," by Amy Winehouse, and "Don't Cha," by Julia Ward and Black Power. This was nothing serious, or so one would think. The problem wasn't how much time I spent in the gym, but rather how much time I spent outside the gym obsessing over it. Whether it was vaulting over my couch or using the rug in the den as a floor exercise, I was enchanted by every aspect of the sport. I would force my mom to let me stay an extra twenty minutes,

6   "BBC News | EUROPE | Romanian Gymnasts Faked Age To Compete." *News.Bbc.Co.Uk.* (2002).

minimum, to watch the team practice after my class was over. My mom didn't mind as she had always wanted to be a gymnast when she was a child, so surely this was scratching her itching obsession with the sport as well. This shared love for the sport connected us in more ways than one throughout my life.

Before long, a team coach plucked me from my recreational class one week. Her name was Victoria, but she told me I could call her Coach Vicky. She had on dark blue velvet sweatpants and a white tank top that read "Phoenix Gymnastics" in one corner and "Coach Vicky" in the other. She pulled me aside and made me try various skills on various events, skills no one else in my class was doing quite yet. I was flattered. She thought I could be one of the team gymnasts, the *real* gymnasts. After the class, Coach Vicky walked me out into the lobby to talk to my mom about signing me up to be on the team. My mom was sold on the idea, most likely because of the overjoyed look on my face. Just like that, I was one of the team gymnasts.

My first day of practice as a rising level-four gymnast was thrilling. There was no holding back anymore. My eye was on the prize, which was constantly changing as I learned new skills and advanced onto the harder ones. Some girls became frustrated as the skills became harder to master. Others began to give up and their attendance at practice dwindled. Others even quit outright, not feeling the intense commitment required was worth the return. I, on the other hand, loved being a gymnast. The challenge was intoxicating and the time investment was thoroughly pleasing. I was hooked; I was sure of that.

By the time I was five, I spent more time at the white, cinder block walled gym and less time in the other sports I had been enrolled in. I could be found doing cartwheels on the soccer field and wearing my gymnastics leotards to dance class. I didn't quit any of the other sports that I was currently in, since my mom told me, "you never quit something midway through, you always finish out your commitments." I definitely didn't want to be a quitter, so when the end of each of the sports seasons came, I did not re-enroll. Instead, I completely and entirely immersed myself in gymnastics.

* * *

I knew this was starting to become a sole focus in my life when my time spent in the gym doubled and then tripled. Before I knew it, I was spending six days at practice and the seventh day was a private lesson with Coach Vicky to work on whatever skill needed the most attention that week. Coach Vicky lived down the block from my house, so she would come and pick me up before my private lesson. She would get to my house a little early to go in and chat with my mom for a bit because my mom was the head of the team parents committee. Then we would leave for Dunkin' Donuts and Coach Vicky would get a large iced coffee with milk and two sugars and I would get a chocolate frosted donut, which she swore me to secrecy about indulging in, and I would eat it on the way to the gym. It was the routine.

We had the whole gym to ourselves on Sunday mornings and we would practice for almost two hours. "The harder the work, the better you'll be," Coach Vicky's words echoed in the empty gymnastics facility. My mom would come to watch about thirty minutes into the private lesson. Sometimes, she would sit in the gym with us, although during practice she would never be allowed to do that. About fifteen minutes before one of my teammates would arrive for their private lesson, my mom would go sit in the lobby, since no one else's mom was allowed the privilege of ever sitting in the gym to watch their daughter's private lesson. I was close with Coach Vicky and she was good friends with my mom as well. She was only twenty-four years old, so she saw my mom as a mentor and, as she unwaveringly declared every Sunday during our private lesson, "Serena is my honorary daughter."

When age seven rolled around, I was finally eligible to compete. With that came another routine: all the girls came over the afternoon before the meet for our twisties hairstyle, then a big bowl of pasta, a long, restful night of sleep, bagels the morning of, and, finally, my mom's pep talk on the way to the competition. It was the same routine before every meet; it became the norm. If we were far from home, everyone would gather in our hotel room for twisties, then off to an Italian restaurant for pasta, good night's sleep, bagels in the morning, and mom's pep talk on the way there. It became comforting to know what to expect.

* * *

It was not uncommon to be in the gym for this many hours a day, nearly every day of the week. Especially not for gymnasts who had high expectations of their career.

In 2008, Jordyn Wieber, who later became a 2012 Olympic gold medalist, was interviewed and the conversation was posted on the USA Gymnastics blog:

"Q: How many hours a week do you train? Walk me through your daily routine.

Jordyn: I train about 30 hours each week. Three days a week I have two practices a day so seven hours total of training. I go to the gym in the morning around 8 a.m. to 10:30, then I go to school from 11 to 2:30 and then I go back to the gym."[7]

---

7   "Catching up with Jordyn Wieber and Kamerin Moore." *USA Gymnastics.* (2008).

* * *

After five months of competing, we attended the Mother of Pearl meet. This gym smelled different, fresher. The music was more regal than our typical workout radio station. It made the day feel more important; it made me feel more important. During warm-ups, I was feeling really good about my routines. I was spot on with every skill, especially on beam. We had our long warm-ups and then we all walked outside of the arena before the introductions and national anthem. I was especially excited for today and I had a really good feeling about my routines.

We started the meet on beam. We had a quick touch warm-up and off to the races we went. I was first up so I was going to set the tone for the entire meet. I was feeding off the energy of my teammates cheering me on and could see all of our parents and siblings sitting in the bleachers cheering loudly too. The combination of the relieving satisfaction knowing everyone had faith in me and the adrenaline pumping through my veins knowing I worked hard enough in practice to master my routine under pressure was intoxicating.

The judge saluted me and that was my signal to start. Once I saluted back, I drowned out every noise of the outside world. It was just me and the beam for the sixty seconds of my routine. I took every skill as an individual feat, presenting poise and attitude in the dance transitioning between the skills. Before I knew it, I was dismounting with a perfect stick. I saluted the judge with a smile from ear to ear and the noise of the outside world quickly began to pour in again. Coach Vicky came running over to give me a hug and the rest of my teammates were right behind her. I was sure it was the best routine I had ever done.

The rest of the meet went well too. I was pleased with all of my routines, but I was especially pleased with my performance on beam. We gathered around our gym bags in the corner of the arena, all chatting about how we felt the meet went. We weren't sure where we fell in the standings quite yet, since Coach Vicky didn't let us watch other gym's gymnasts as she told us that would be a distraction. We dressed in our Phoenix Gymnastics warm-up suits and huddled around the awards podium. Vault first, then bars, and then my favorite, the beam. They went from fifth place up to first place. I sat patiently with my fingers crossed in my pockets, hoping I had secured the number one spot.

"And in first place from Phoenix Gymnastics, Serena Pergola." I had done it! And that very feeling that flooded into me that afternoon is why fifteen years later, I am still intoxicated by this sport. A feeling that stems from pride, satisfaction and passion culminating in an undying addiction I will never shake.

* * *

All gymnasts start with the same mindset, "Gymnastics is my whole life, and I dream of going to the Olympics and being a world champ."[8]

* * *

The addiction became even more intoxicating as time went on. At twelve years old in the seventh grade, I was recruited to be a member of the Bethpage high school varsity gymnastics team. I was much younger than the rest of the team, but I had ample experience as a gymnast due to club gymnastics, so they were excited to be adding my skills to the roster. I joined the team, invigorated by their interest in my skill level. I did, however, have to adapt to the maturity level of my teammates who were much older than me. I already was a year younger than those in my grade, having gone to school a year early, but now I was three to six years younger than all of my teammates. This had potential to pose a big challenge in terms of adaptation, but being at Phoenix surrounded by the older girls constantly, I was able to adapt quite quickly and soon became friends with many of the girls. With this newfound sense of team camaraderie and increase in the

---

8   Raisman, A. *Fierce: How Competing for Myself Changed Everything.* Little, Brown Books for Young Readers. (2018).

team's level of skill set, the once struggling Bethpage team rose once again to many victories.

At thirteen years old, now in the eighth grade, I helped set a school-record high, all-around score, winning the Nassau County team championship in the regular season. It was a very exciting and rewarding season to be a part of. Not only had I developed a close bond with my teammates, but I got rather close to my coaches as well, specifically Coach Kim.

Kim was the kindest and most encouraging coach I had ever come to know. She was everyone's number one fan, offering unparalleled support every step of every routine. I loved competing for her team because of her genuine appreciation for every single person on the team. It didn't matter if your contribution was on every single line up, competing in the all-around and scoring the highest scores on every event or if you set up the mats for your teammates and cheered them on from the sidelines, to Kim we all were of very special value. I found this to be an admirable approach in a sport that rarely put emphasis on team camaraderie. It married the idea of an individual sport with a team collaboration.

High school varsity gymnastics was very different than club gymnastics for me. Similar to Kim's team approach, it was much less about my individual performance, and much more about the team's performance overall. I did not see my routines as me completing them for myself, but rather every time I saluted the judge, I focused on performing to the best of my ability to contribute the most to the team. This gave me a newfound love for gymnastics in a very different way. It fueled my passion to become a collegiate gymnast even more than ever before. The new song booming from the radio was the instrumental version of "Rock You Like a Hurricane," by Scorpions, while I tumbled down the corners and danced strikingly around the floor. There was nothing more exciting than knowing my scores were helping to bring about team victories. Even if I had my best meet on an individual scale, if the team did not perform well overall, I considered it an unsuccessful day. I stood on the sidelines, cheering on my teammates unwaveringly until my turn came to contribute my best. We rushed the mat every time someone finished a routine to ensure that they felt honored for the hard work they were contributing to our team.

* * *

"When you come together and do really well as a team, it creates this amazing bond that you share with your teammates for the rest of your life." Raisman wrote.[9]

* * *

---

9   Reed, B. "Aly Raisman On the Importance of the Team Competition." *Flogymnastics.Com.* (2015).

2011 brought about many team victories, including a conference championship. It also brought me many personal victories as I was named a member of the 2011 All-Long-Island gymnasts of the year and granted a spot on the New York State team for varsity gymnastics. I was honored to compete in the all-around. My parents and grandparents all piled in my car on the way to Albany, New York where the state competition was to be held. I knew it was an extra special meet because my grandparents rarely came to see me compete. My grandma would get too nervous that I would get hurt so she would cringe before every one of my routines and my grandpa, on the other hand, didn't really understand the skills. Nonetheless, they always supported me unwaveringly and I was particularly excited to show off my hard work on a statewide stage.

Little did I know this would be the devastating beginning of the end of my gymnastics career.

* * *

Yet even from the other side of the glass, to this day, I have an undying addiction to the sport of gymnastics.

CHAPTER 2

THE BREAK THAT CHANGED MY LIFE

———

The 2011 New York State championship meet had begun and I had solid warm-ups and was feeling really good about my routines that day.

* * *

Leading up to this meet, I had landed on my neck too many times and my neck could barely make a full right turn. My back felt as though there were sprains all down either side and my ankles ached with every step I took. My wrists cracked every time I turned my hand in a circle and my Achilles burned every time I pointed my toes. Nonetheless, these feelings were all deemed "normal," considering the nature of the sport I chose to blindly fall in love with. All things aside, my body felt "strong"—well, what a gymnast would consider strong following thirty plus hours a week of pounding incessantly.

* * *

We were starting the meet on vault, one of my least favorite events. I had struggled for a long time to successfully master my Yurchenko, but finally the time had come that the skill had become second nature to me. I stood at the end of the runway and saluted the judge, zoning out the booming cheers throughout the arena. I stared down the runway at the vault that was 44.6 feet in front of me. I raised my heels up off the ground, adrenaline coursing through my veins. I began my sprint down the runway, feeling particularly powerful; lunged impeccably; placed my hands down onto the mat just where they needed to be; flipped over the round-off reaching back for the vault in the backward arch position; *crack*; turned over the handspring, lifting into flight off the vault in the tucked position; two full rotations and a stuck landing. I saluted the judge, fighting off every urge in my body to allow the imminent pain that I was in to spread across my face and fall to the floor in defeat.

* * *

I heard the crack. It sounded so loud I began to wonder if anyone else heard it too. I hope not, then I can't hide that it happened. I will not be the problem. I will finish this meet. A knife-like, stabbing pain dragged down my spine and into my right leg. I stuck the landing by the grace of God himself. A forced smile spread across my face as I turned to salute the judges. I will not be the problem. I will finish this meet. I see Kim running toward me, hands up ready to high-five me. I matched her excitement. I could see her lips moving, but I heard no words coming out. I must zone back in, but the pain was all-encompassing. I will not be the problem. I will finish this meet.

* * *

"Let me go get my grips so I can get ready for bars." I uttered to Kim. She sensed something was wrong by my complacency and her eyes followed as my right leg lagged just a moment behind the rest of my body.

"Are you hurt?" Kim put her hand on my shoulder to turn me back around.

* * *

Another stabbing sensation sent down my spine, settling in my right leg. I will not be the problem. I will finish this meet.

* * *

"No. I just rolled my ankle a little on the landing. I'll ice it while I wait for bars. It's no big deal." I lied through my teeth. Kim hesitantly nodded and walked over to the trainer to get me a bag of ice.

The trainer rushed over with a bag of ice ready and asked me to sit so she could evaluate my ankle to be sure I was healthy enough to continue with the competition. I hadn't hurt my ankle, so I knew she would give me the green light to continue to compete and I didn't resist her evaluation. I glanced over to the bleachers where my parents and grandparents were sitting. My mom shot me a look that read "suck it up." The classic gymnastics world response—do not be the problem. There is no pain bad enough to rationalize not finishing a competition, or so I was made out to believe from the age of three.

As I sat on a mat with my ankle hanging over the edge, I nodded, half listening to the trainer's suggestions. I strapped my grips on tight, pinching the skin on my wrist just enough to attempt to draw some of my brain's attention to another part of my body. This did not work.

* * *

This pain was nothing like I had ever felt before. My back has been hurting for months now, but this was different. The pain usually came in rushes. This pain was consistent and stronger than I had ever felt before. My right leg felt numb and was hard to move. I will not be the problem. I will finish this meet.

* * *

I drifted through the competition, half conscious and in imminent pain. Kim kept checking in on my ankle, making sure the pain wasn't increasing. I felt bad for lying, but I guess I wasn't really lying by saying my ankle didn't hurt, since I couldn't even feel my ankle for it to hurt. Finally, we finished the competition. I had a less than mediocre performance and I could tell it had really irritated my parents as they both sat in the bleachers giving me the "what the hell was that?" look.

I received half-hearted congratulations from both of my parents as we headed to the parking lot to file into the car. We went to PF Chang's for dinner with my grandparents, who both thought I did great of course because they had no idea what my routines were supposed to look like. We sat down to eat and I was very quiet and kept claiming it was because I was tired. My parents were both frustrated, assuming I was quiet because I was disappointed with my performance.

My dad reached his arm around me and patted my back, half-heartedly reassuring me that I would "do better next time." As his hand made contact with my back, I screamed.

Both of my parents shot a look of death at me, embarrassed by my behavior, especially in a restaurant. Tears rushed down my face and my mom declared we would be excusing ourselves to use the bathroom.

As we walked over to the bathroom, I went from crying to sobbing uncontrollably, barely able to breathe let alone talk. My mom was getting increasingly more frustrated, clenching her teeth and telling me to get it together.

"I broke my back." I finally pushed out between sobs.

"What are you talking about?" My mom confusedly uttered back.

"I heard it crack during my vault. I broke my back. You need to call the doctor. My right leg has been numb all day." I wiped my face and started taking deep breaths.

"Serena, what are you talking about? You competed the entire meet knowing you broke your back? Why?" She visibly softened her furious face.

"Because I was not going to be the problem. There is no pain bad enough to rationalize not finishing a competition so I sucked it up." I declared proudly, meanwhile I was keeled over in pain by this point.

"This is the exception! Okay, let me go get my phone. I will make some phone calls." She headed back to the table, the color completely washed from her face, clearly stunned by the information I had just let her in on.

The whole drive back home was fairly quiet. No one really knew what to say to me. I sprawled out across the third row of seats, wailing intermittently, spazzing uncontrollably as the stabbing continuously spread from my spine to my legs. From this day on, my life would never be the same. My new level of "pain-free" was a consistent stabbing pain stretching from my spine down my right leg.

* * *

Three days later we went to a spine specialist. He ordered an X-ray and MRI, concluding I had Spondylolisthesis, and two bulging discs, something he deemed "uncommon for a thirteen-year-old, but not uncommon for a gymnast." As he went into detail about what these diagnoses would mean for me, there was only one thing on my mind.

"I know this is a lot to take in. Do you have any questions at this point?" The doctor consoled.

"Can I still do gymnastics?" I blurted out.

The doctor began to laugh, slowly realizing I wasn't kidding. "Yes, I suppose. We will have to re-evaluate after three months in the back brace. Let's take this step-by-step." He finally responded.

"Okay, so I can still do gymnastics then?" My one-track mind blurted out again.

"As it stands right now, that answer is maybe." He shot a look at my mom who was turning red with embarrassment. Maybe wasn't a no, so I heard, *"Yes, if you work hard enough."* Hard work was all I knew, so that was easy enough.

* * *

I spent the next three months on the couch barely able to breathe or move and in constant pain, unparalleled by any pain I had ever felt before in my life. Nothing subsided it, not the pain pills, not ice packs, not heating pads, not an Epsom salt bath, nothing. I watched the Food Network and gymnastics clips for days on end, but every day passed, slowly dragging on. I was bored and frustrated, and in immense pain.

Meanwhile, my body took this opportunity to undergo puberty, which was definitely the icing on the cake for me. My breasts grew three sizes, so much so that I was pouring out of my clothes and we had to go out and buy all new bras.

I got my period, which definitely wasn't pleasant. And worst of all, I grew three inches. And I say worst of all because gymnasts want to stay prepubescent and petite or all of their skills become triple as hard to learn.

* * *

"Without sounding condescending to young women, this is a little girl's sport," Geddert said. "With their body changes and the wear-and-tear everybody goes through, once they become women, it just becomes very, very difficult."[10]

* * *

Three months later I was postpuberty and post-back brace. I began physical therapy, which meant I began mastering the art of lying through my pain. I spent every day claiming I felt significantly better and Laura, my physical therapist, remained completely unfazed by my lies, continuing me on the regular program and not speeding up the process like I had hoped my lying would grant me. It was horrible. I was fighting through immense amounts of pain and stabbing sensations through my spine and legs, all with a smile on my face. We concluded each session the same exact way, "Can I go back to gymnastics yet?" I would beg.

---

10 Phillips, I. "A Gymnastics Coach Explains Why Female Gymnasts Are So Young." *INSIDER.* (2016).

"Not quite. You are improving, but you are not quite there yet." Laura would reply. Laura was a trooper though, she never got frustrated with me, but rather she understood the level of frustration I was experiencing.

She tried to ease me into the belief that collegiate gymnastics may not be in the cards for me any longer.

I didn't believe her though. No matter how many times she would ease me into the conversation, she always ended up reluctantly accepting my stubborn response of, "I am feeling much better though. I am going to be back in the gym in no time, which will still give me plenty of time to earn a scholarship and compete in college. I know it will be hard work, but I know I can do it." I would declare as I hopped off the table, fighting every urge to burst out into tears with the level of pain I was experiencing.

* * *

A few months later, I had a check-in with my doctor. I had trained myself not to wince when someone touched the area of the fracture so that he would clear me to begin gymnastics again. I was getting anxious watching everyone improve on their skills and feeling like I was falling way behind. I passed the test, partially because I had convinced him that I was feeling much better, but most likely because he didn't want to deal with my reaction if he said I needed more time, or worse, I couldn't go back at all.

Medical clearance was my free pass to bliss. I headed back into practice that very night, wincing and screeching under my breath in my bedroom as I pulled on my leotard. The second I stepped foot in the gym, I could feel a weight lift off my shoulders and a light reignite inside of me, but the stabbing sensation was right behind the rush of excitement to remind me that this would not be an easy feat.

Months of endless hours in the gym, building my strength, then reteaching my body the basic skills and finally working up to new skills. It was grueling and extremely taxing on my body, but I knew it would be worth the stress. The second I left the gym every night, the adrenaline would rush out of my body, I had to fight every urge inside of me to burst into tears and never walk back into the gym again. Not only were the skills harder to master due to my undergoing of puberty, but the level of pain I was in was unmatched by anything I had ever experienced in my life. I couldn't show weakness though, or they would pull me. They meaning everyone: my parents, my coaches, my doctor, my physical therapist; I was under close watch and I wouldn't let them take away my final chance at collegiate gymnastics.

Finally, I had lied so often to everyone around me, that I began to believe my lie myself. I had convinced myself that the consistent stabbing sensation was my new measure of "pain-free." Just the stabbing sensation meant I could continue practice, but stabbing sensation and numbness in my legs, tell my coaches and revert back to just strengthening exercises. That was my new normal; only no one knew it besides me.

I decided that if I wanted to become a high-level collegiate gymnast and earn a scholarship, I needed to switch gyms and go to the most competitive one in Long Island. This was a hard decision because it meant I would need to leave all of my teammates, and more importantly all of my friends. By this point, however, many of my original friends had no longer been doing gymnastics due to injury, lost interest, or otherwise.

So, I made the switch to Gold Medal. This was a very different environment than what I had been used to. A serious emphasis was put on your skill level and an even more serious emphasis was put on your body image. I was shocked and honored when the head coach took an interest in me. It was glaringly obvious that I was far behind the rest of my teammates in terms of skill level, but she took a deep interest in my "pristine lines." Because of those lines, every skill I performed, particularly on beam, looked flawlessly clean and graceful, yet powerful and purposeful. She spoke a lot about how my body type was "ideal" for gymnastics. This made me feel very special, but it also made me very paranoid of losing this "ideal body." I spent ample time outside of the gym analyzing everything I put into my body which ultimately resulted in skipping meals and replacing food with an abundance of water.

She also took an interest in helping me to succeed in landing a scholarship to a top collegiate gymnastics program. I visited schools such as the University of North Carolina Chapel Hill and the University of Maryland College Park where they tried to "woo" me into choosing their program, offering me not only scholarships, but clothing and other spirited attire. I was impressed to say the least, but I was more focused on making sure a smile remained plastered across my face so the coaches would not be able to tell the level of pain I was experiencing just simply walking around the campus.

As I returned from the campus visits, filled with a passion for collegiate gymnastics even stronger than I originally had, I began to push myself even harder in the gym attempting to master high level skills in a short amount of time. The pain had gotten increasingly worse and I had to let my mom in on my struggle. She began scheduling appointments for acupuncture, cupping, deep tissue massages, and ordering expensive natural medicines in support of my collegiate gymnastics ambition.

Eventually, I fell way too far behind my teammates at Gold Medal, continuously injuring new parts of my body as a result of my back not being able to sustain the pounding and stress that I was putting it under on a daily basis. I gave up my spot at the gym mid-season and found myself back with my friends and teammates. Feeling slightly defeated, the perk was definitely being back with my friends. The only problem was, most of them had suffered serious injuries of their own and were no longer in the sport themselves.

After much tribulation and escalating stabbing sensations, I mastered enough skills to compete in what would be my last meet, though I did not know it at the time. I had a flexible back brace strapped around my waist and I winced every step of the way, but I was determined and I let the adrenaline of being back out on the competition floor overcome the pain.

* * *

Unfortunately, the inevitable finally caught up to me. Somehow, I still managed to be the problem. After two years of fighting with every last ounce of me to remain a competitive gymnast, I found myself on the doctor's table replaying his words over and over in my head, *"You cannot continue doing gymnastics. If you continue doing this you may never walk again. You may never be able to carry a child. You will never live a normal life. This is something that goes far beyond just the next couple of years. The damage you have done to your back is permanent."* Permanent. Now there was a word that scared the very little light I had left inside of me. There was plenty more he said, but that was all I heard.

* * *

And just like that, all of my hopes, dreams, and aspirations were shattered on the floor in front of me and the world went dark.

CHAPTER 3

FINDING MY
FOREVER FRIENDS

"We're going to Bean's tonight, right?"

It became so routine that the question wasn't even regularly asked, it was assumed.

* * *

There were two classifications of friends for me growing up: my school friends and my gymnastics friends.

I had school friends because they were in my classes, but they would get angry at me and end up lashing out when I said I couldn't have play dates as often as they wanted to due to having gymnastics practice. They didn't necessarily mean to leave me out, it just became assumed that I wouldn't be able to come and, therefore, I got invited less and less.

Then, there were my gymnastics friends. To them, this rule did not seem to apply. They exceeded any expectation I could ever have of them. They supported me through anything and everything. A huge part of why I loved being in the gym was because the girls I was in the gym with made it all the more fun.

* * *

"You got this Bean!"

"The beam queen at it again!"

"Come on Bean!"

Their ear-piercing cheers and warm words of encouragement kept me going for the better part of my gymnastics career. My nickname, Bean, was derived from "serene bean the beam queen." I was the only one on the team who really loved the beam, everyone else strongly preferred the other three events. Gaining new skills and winning meets would not have been nearly as rewarding without these girls by my side.

Together, we underwent the earth-shattering (we were ten, keep things in perspective) change of our childhood coach moving and no longer coaching us anymore. We all diverted to a new gym to continue practicing together, but now there were other girls on our team. Things were different, but our bond remained unwaveringly strong.

As for outside the gym, we did everything together. From watching college and Olympic gymnastics meets in my living room to spending hours in my hot tub and pool until we legitimately became human raisins.

* * *

We all had a favorite Olympic gymnast, mine being Carly Patterson and Shawn Johnson because they were beam wizards, and we shared a love for University of Florida college gymnastics as we all wanted to have the Gator clap in our floor routines. We daydreamed about all of us attending the same college and cheering each other on from the side of the mat. We ate more food than should have been humanly possible to consume for children our age, and then we would go back for second and third servings. We laughed for hours on no end and we cried when we would get injured or have mental blocks.

"Bean, you're going to do your floor routine like that?! You are such a goof!"

"That's okay you will heal soon enough and be back out here kicking butt before you know it."

"You have this. Just trust in yourself and you will nail the skill. You've been practicing for months now and you are ready. Let's do this!"

We would celebrate the good practices with trips to La Piazza and Cugini, the pizzerias near my house, and we would shake off the bad ones with encouraging talks to bring a positive attitude to the next practice. Countless away meets with seven-hour car rides and visits to every diner within a twenty-mile radius of the arena resulted in our seven families becoming one family.

* * *

Ranging from ages three to five when we met, there are seven girls who became my best friends in my first three years of gymnastics that still to this day, have had my back through anything and everything. I genuinely know that every single one of them are just one phone call away if I need them and it is an extremely comforting feeling.

Each of them is unique and fulfills a different aspect of friendship for me.

"Let's wear our pink and blue tie dye dresses on Saturday, okay? And then we will play Bratz after we get home. Deal?"

There is Jordan. She was my first friend of the group and we were completely inseparable for ten years. I am talking "matching outfits, finishing each other's sentences, play dates every day, sleepovers every night with my mom dropping her off at school the next morning" type of inseparable. We would have top secret play dates where we would play Bratz in my basement and not tell anyone else about it. We had an entire world set up for these dolls, changing their outfits every day and concocting elaborate life stories for each of them. The funny thing is, I think we spent more time setting up scenes for the dolls than we ever spent actually playing with them, but nonetheless we had a blast. We spent every waking moment together from age four to age fourteen. As we grew older, she wasn't the biggest fan of hugs, or really affection altogether. Contradictory to that, I am what most people call a "hugger." She always lets me show her my affection and reciprocates my hugs. She is one of the toughest people I know, but she has a heart filled with love.

"This was the best birthday of MY LIFE. I love being 21. We went to lunch and the place had closed down and a HOOT-ERS opened up in its place. Can you BELIEVE that?! Then we went to a bar at night and it turned out that night was Drag Queen night. Could it have gotten more PERFECT?!"

There is Brooke. She makes me laugh at any time of any day. Her extroverted, rambunctious, genuinely hilarious spirit brightens every room she walks into. Her strength and resilience in life is unmatched. Life has thrown some tough battles at her and yet she carries on with grace. This is not to say she never needs an ear to listen or a helping hand, but somehow, she always manages to find the good in the bad and persist onward. She knows just when you need a pick-me-up and provides it effortlessly and selflessly. We have shared numerous late-night calls of raw venting and I wouldn't want to have anyone else on the other end of the phone.

"Did you know your name backwards is Aneres Alogrep."

There is Danielle. She is intelligent and humorous. Her humor is unprompted, it is intrinsic in who she is. Her intelligence is so apparent, it comes out in the oddest instances. It rolls off her tongue as if it was normal, yet so she is the only person in the world who would be unprompted and think of that. Moments of raw thought verbalized are the epitome of her humor and I love every minute of them she shares with me.

"Guysssss we are the best friends ever I love it."

There is Jordyn. There is no one word to describe her. She is so true to herself it is inspiring. She proudly and authentically takes on every aspect of her life, never wavering from her values. She has made the best in every situation of life and she loves to inform us of all the wacky things others in her life do. She is random and spontaneous, yet down-to-earth and loyal. This loyalty is what is so wonderfully authentic about her.

"You have to go blue. Then we can go blue together. Bean!!"

There is Courtney. She has no idea just how fantastic she is. She is quiet and curious, intelligent and dynamic, and extremely caring and generous. When I visited her at the University of Michigan her freshman year, she seemed so comfortable outside of her comfort zone. It was refreshing and yet soothing. She made Ann Arbor feel like home before I had even committed to come to school here. Her reserved manner and unmatched kind heart are what make her a gem.

"GUYS THE EIFFEL TOWER."

There is Jordan, better known as JM. She is the baby of the group. I have always seen her as the little sister I never had. We used to play jokes on her when we were young, telling her wild things like a toy model of the Eiffel Tower that sat on top of a building in Long Island City was the real one from Paris and they moved it here, or that we were crossing the Nile River in the middle of upstate New York, or better yet that she would be having a Bat Mitzvah even though she was Catholic. They were all harmless jokes, but we loved to fool her and then watch her full-bellied laugh at us when she would find out the truth. We did still celebrate her "Bat Mitzvah" with a cruise when she turned thirteen, so I guess not all of the jokes were bad. She is a fighter. Suffering numerous injuries, she never quit searching for a sport to pursue. She has a competitive drive like no other. Her eyes captivate you from the moment you look at her and her heart is bigger than the ocean. She truly is the little sister I never had.

"Serena let's have Notorious Pink and hang out!"

Last, but definitely not least, there is Alexa. She is absolutely hilarious without even trying and extremely genuine, always making you feel loved. She is reserved when you first meet her, but when she gets to know you, you so graciously get to know her as well. We shared a "three-month sleepover" in a studio apartment one summer in Manhattan. It was both of our first times living in Manhattan and I wouldn't have wanted to take on the adventure with anyone else. Countless wine nights in the apartment watching Friends and reflecting on stories of college and various bars and restaurants tried and true with delicious meals and great laughs. The experience was definitely one that I would not have traded for the world and, most of all, would not have wanted to share with anyone besides her.

* * *

They supported me through the injury that changed my life and they still support me every single day through every new obstacle and adventure I am faced with. I never have to feel alone and I am truly blessed to have not just one or two, but seven girls who will truly be my friends forever.

* * *

"We love you, Bean. You'll get through this and we'll be by your side the entire time."

And sure enough, they have been.

CHAPTER 4

THE SMILE ISN'T ALWAYS INDICATIVE OF HAPPINESS

———

One specific forever friend connects with me on a more intimate level. We both struggle with body image and anxiety. This is not a connection either of us are particularly thrilled about. Nonetheless, it is nice to have someone there to not only support you, but to understand what you are feeling.

My ally in this battle is Brooke.

Brooke has the biggest personality, filling every room with booming laughter and a sparkling smile. She carries a presence unparalleled by any other individual. All of this, you would never expect from a 4'11" petite young woman.

She shared with me what her daily battle is like fighting anxiety. She was raw and honest, unraveling the inner workings of this complicated mental health battle. I admire how incredibly strong and brave she was in sharing these thoughts with me and allowing me to include them here to share with you all. Here is a little look behind the curtain of body image anxiety and how it oftentimes influences various aspects of your life in a very particular way.

* * *

She finds herself standing in front of a mirror, regretting the fact that she will never look like she did when she was ten years old. Less than proud of her thin arms, carved abs, and narrow legs. Others look at her in awe, jealous of her physique. But to her, this physique will never match the rock-solid core, jacked arms, and powerful legs she had at a mere ten years old. She details herself as "manly-looking" at the age of thirteen because her shoulders were bigger than her hips, never having gone through the normal transition of puberty. A gymnast of twelve years feeling an incessant need to be muscular, as the more muscle you have, the better you would be. That is what she was told, constantly, naggingly, tossed out as a compliment that she had this solid physique.

Emphasis was placed on the way the leotard fit your body like a glove, one lump and you were not considered a successful gymnast. Words like "lazy" or "recreational" were used to describe those that did not have perfectly cut muscles. Natural competitiveness was ingrained in her; however, it was amplified by constantly being forced to compare herself to the person next to her.

"Perfection was the farfetched, unattainable goal at all times."

"I was never the best on the team," she recalls, "but I was always working the absolute hardest I could, giving my all at every practice."

Looking back, there are so many things she wishes she could say to her younger self. Hands bracing the shoulders of her young self, reminding her that getting stronger does not validate her; there is more to life than just physical strength. She finds it very problematic that coaches would stress that the basics of gymnastics were so essential, yet she was never taught those basics. The basics are the fundamental makeup of the sport and they lay the groundwork for every skill you learn throughout the rest of your gymnastics career. By these basics not being taught with the utmost importance and precision, the higher-level skills become increasingly more challenging to master. Instead of the women that she looked up to only because of their physical strength, she wishes her role models had been those with strong basics who moved gracefully through the more challenging skills.

As a young adult, now out of the sport due to injury, she reflects on how gymnastics has translated into various aspects of her life. Society says everything is all about numbers. The Rio 2016 Olympic Gymnastics Team ranged from 102 to 115 pounds, stretching from 4'8" to 5'2".[11] These women were sixteen to twenty-two years old. And yet Brooke, very much so in this same height and weight range as these Olympic level athletes, does not feel as though her body is something to be proud of. A constant feeling that everyone is watching her at all times, analyzing her every move. The individuality of the sport made the team dynamics during practice seem like numerous eyes of judgement at times. This need for approval and appraisal in every relationship she holds in her life is a result of constant judgement from the age of only three.

She believes shame is rooted in self-talk. We convince ourselves that others are constantly judging us. Society says shame is a negative, meanwhile society is usually who imposed these negative thoughts on us through the media depicting their form of "perfection." Constantly being told she was not enough has seeped into her self-talk. One slipup and she feels as though she is not successful.

---

11   "Gymnastics." *Teamusa.Org.* (2019).

The fact that, "it isn't what you look like, but how you use your body to your advantage that actually is important," rings through her head constantly throughout her time recovering. She is healthy and has good endurance and she has decided that this should be her focus. Her hardworking nature shining through in her everyday life has helped guide her to achieving her goals.

* * *

Aly Raisman recounts an episode following a 2010 meet in Italy, where she won her first all-around title. At the banquet afterwards, a USAG staffer called her out for eating a slice of pizza. "Aly, you are never allowed to do that again, as long as you're competing," the unnamed staff person said. Raisman called her mother in tears, worried a slice of pizza would prevent her from being chosen for another national team."[12]

Proof that even high-profile women are struggling with the same body image issues as us.

* * *

Brooke's experiences may not sound all that different to a fellow former gymnast, or even current gymnast, or honestly

---

12 Corbett, S. "Olympic Gymnast Aly Raisman's Memoir Holds Painful Revelations." *Publishersweekly.Com.* (2017).

most young adults today. Unfortunately, body image anxiety is all too common. My personal struggle is balancing healthfulness and overindulgence. I try not to restrict myself too much or when I do have a day of indulgence, I overindulge. Similarly, I try not to be too strict all of the time or I get overly conscious and count every ounce of indulgence as a complete loss. Moderation is the clear best choice, but it always seems to be easier said than done.

This concept of moderation is still something I struggle with to this day. I go through waves of cutting carbs completely from my diet or indulging daily because "I deserve it." I do not have a fully formed and practiced solution to this struggle quite yet; however, I do know that recognizing the problem and admitting it to myself is the first step. I pay conscious attention to my internal obsessive thoughts regarding my eating habits and I am proud of myself for being able to recognize when I am being irrationally strict. This is a process and I am very much still undergoing the process, but what I will say is this: Embrace and love your body, for it fights every battle you go through fiercely.

One other thing I try to do every morning is tell myself one positive trait about myself. It can be something simple such as my hair looks pretty today or I love this outfit on me, or something more internal such as I am going to kill this meeting today or I am really strong for staying positive through this really negative time in my life. A little personal pick-me-up is refreshing. This taps directly into my mindfulness routine in empowering myself to be the best me that I can be. I firmly believe I make a choice every morning whether I want to take my hardships out on others or I want to accept my hardships and battle them fiercely. There are days where this decision is much harder than others, especially when my hardships are really weighing me down, but the more I consciously make the choice to battle them fiercely, the lighter they seem to get. While healthfulness definitely goes far beyond physical being, I find that my mental being is a little easier to maintain when my physical one is in a good place.

Most of all, positivity is so important. This goes for both my physical and my mental being. The dark days seem to always be filled with negativity, but don't let that dull your light. Be happy in your own skin and celebrate yourself. There is only one you in this world which means you can be the best you.

CHAPTER 5

THE SAD TRUTH THAT ALL I'LL EVER BE IS JUST A GYMNAST

"You are now 21 with the back of an 81-year-old."

No, that isn't me trying to be funny. Those words are directly from my doctor's mouth.

This was my worst nightmare. I was second best, an almost college gymnast. I put in all of the hard work to receive a gold medal, and all I got was silver.

* * *

Let me back it up a little.

"Serena, what are you talking about? You competed the entire meet knowing you broke your back? Why?" She visibly softened her furious face.

"Because I was not going to be the problem. There is no pain bad enough to rationalize not finishing a competition so I sucked it up." I declared proudly, meanwhile I was keeled over in pain by this point.

Remember that?

* * *

By this point I'm sure you know I absolutely love the sport of gymnastics. Not only was it intoxicating to do the sport, it is intoxicating to watch the sport. The raw power and talent you must embody to truly master the skills is an art. That being said, I also recognize the culture of gymnastics and how it has shaped my life, both positively and negatively.

Without gymnastics, I had a void and I was yearning for it to be filled. My quick fix involved exploring diving as another sport that mimicked some similar body positions. I had hoped that by tricking my muscles into thinking I was still doing gymnastics moves, I could trick my heart into feeling whole again. As you may have assumed, this did not happen. The void grew. This led me to feel even more empty. I began to worry: Is it true that all I would ever be is just a gymnast?

"However, what many people don't realize is that extended participation in gymnastics classes also provides many additional cognitive and psychological benefits that will continue to benefit an individual throughout their life."[13]

First let's start with the good that gymnastics gave me. It's always better to bask in the good, at least for a little while. Even more simply, let's start with the uncomplicated good. One example of this, which I previously detailed in depth, is my friends. Those girls truly are my forever friends and without gymnastics to not only bring us together, but bond us like a family, I would not have found them.

Let's not forget what they said:

"We love you, Bean. You'll get through this and we'll be by your side the entire time."

* * *

_____

13   "Benefits of Gymnastics." *Springfit.* (2019).

"Many of the benefits of gymnastics are NOT related to learning gymnastics skills, but more important developmental areas that will help your child become a better student and young adult."[14]

Other examples of good are my: discipline, work ethic, resilience, self-confidence, perseverance, and goal-setting skills. Although it seems like gymnastics has provided me with a lot of positive character traits, they all come with more complicated baggage than they appear to.

"What will help them is the multitude of skills, both physical skills for a healthy lifestyle and personal skills to succeed in school and work, learned from doing gymnastics."[15]

* * *

Discipline is definitely a benefit for a young child in their formative years. I always thrived with structure and direction, finding the most success in the activities that encompassed these qualities. Gymnastics is one of those activities, however, I wonder if there is such a thing as too much discipline? This is an idea I have toyed with a lot as I look back on my first couple of years as a gymnast. The structure and direction

---

14   Burgdorf, T. "Benefits of Gymnastics." *Gymnastics Unlimited.* (2019).
15   "Benefits of Gymnastics." *Champaign Gymnastics Academy.* (2019).

were essential to performing the skills the correct way and in turn advancing to the next level of skills. If you didn't have total discipline, you were at a disadvantage. However, total discipline also instilled a burning desire for perfection.

While I attempted complete discipline, I did not succeed because I was not being taught the basic skills the correct way. Years later, by not having these basic skills mastered seamlessly, I struggled to advance. This meant I would sacrifice good body form to achieve the next level of skills, oftentimes overarching my back. This constant pounding on my body in unnatural ways ultimately lead to injury. This unfortunately is not uncommon for gymnasts as they oftentimes go to all extremes to achieve the next level of skills in the sport.

Work ethic is another benefit for a young child. This unwavering work ethic has proved me right for many years. This also feeds into the ability to focus, as gymnastics is a highly technical sport. To master skills, you must be on high alert at all times. One second of misdirected thought and you could seriously injure yourself. Marry these two with determination and you have a child ready to take on any task. The problem is, while these benefits usually resulted in an increased skill level inside the gym, they also resulted in obsessive behaviors outside the gym. I was working tirelessly and never taking a break for relaxation. This not only left my body more susceptible to injury inside of the gym, but it left my mind running endlessly in search of perfection outside of the gym.

This is not uncommon for gymnasts. Do you recall what Brooke said earlier?

"Perfection was the farfetched, unattainable goal at all times."

Or perhaps, let's reflect on what Aly Raisman said in an interview with Reebok:

"Not only is she refusing to stop at the gymnastics glass ceiling, but she's doing it in a sport that is rooted in perfection itself. 'If you breathe at the wrong second, you could make a mistake,' she says. From pointed toes, to slicked-back buns, and stuck landings, flawlessness is what gets you the gold."[16]

"These gymnasts are held to the standard of perfection, and nothing less. To perform less than what was expected of them would be to forfeit their careers, which to them, meant their very lives...In gymnastics, girls are conditioned to believe that nothing less than perfection is acceptable."[17]

---

16 Mazzo, L. "Aly Raisman On What It's Like to Compete in a Sport That's All About Perfection." *Shape.* (2019).

17 "Thoughts on Aly Raisman's Autobiography, 'Fierce.' " *Teenage Struggles.* (2018).

The all-encompassing, entirely enthralling feeling of achieving near perfection contrasted with the earth-shattering pain of falling short is nothing short of completely heartbreaking.

* * *

Next comes resilience. This involves the concept of moving on from mistakes. If you were at a competition and you did not perform to the best of your ability in one event, you had to leave those ill feelings at that event and move on. This sounds like it could be positive, but the intensity of gymnastics makes it harmful. This has resulted in my being vulnerable to being taken advantage of. When someone does me wrong, I am quick to move on and not carry the ill feelings with me. This is both positive and negative: positive when what they did is not that big of a deal; negative when what they did is inexcusable.

Then there is self-confidence. Confidence is absolutely necessary to perform your skills to the best of your ability and the peak of my confidence came when I was on the beam. It's dangerous not to believe in yourself in this sport. Compassion ties into this as you believe in your teammates and instill this belief in them so they can ultimately believe in themselves without a shed of doubt. This sounds like it would be straightforward; compassion for others is always a positive thing. This type of compassion I had mastered, truly and fully supporting my teammates.

The compassion I lacked, however, was compassion for myself.

This is not a foreign idea for anyone struggling with anxiety. I am hard on myself. I set the unattainable goal of perfection. Nevertheless, when these impossible levels are not reached, I become even more anxious. It is the vicious cycle.

* * *

By contrast, one thing I did not lack was strength, both of the body and of the mind. As Brooke spoke of earlier, strength was a necessity for gymnasts, especially for gymnasts under the strict coaching and direction we were under. Finally, there is attention to detail. Judging gymnastics is all about the minute things that the common person's eye would not see. It's about analyzing the finest details that make a skill either perfect, or less than perfect. To improve, you must hone in on these details to continue improving your scores. While these things all seem to be innocent, coupled with a former gymnast who found her confidence in her successful performances that no longer has the perfectly-defined body she once did, taking pride in other people's judgements of her routines is a recipe for disaster for anyone. But more importantly here in my case, created a growing void that got larger with each passing day.

In regards to eating disorders:

"In the 1992 NCAA survey, 51% of the gymnastics programs that responded reported this illness among its team members, 'a far greater percentage than in any other sport' ('Dying to win' 1994). Unfortunately, the real number is probably even higher."[18]

And, of course, the statistic from the beginning of my book:

"A more recent review of the research indicates that female athletes in judged sports have a 13 percent prevalence of eating disorders, compared to just 3 percent in the general population."[19]

Perseverance is another one of those complex concepts. While it is important to keep fighting on through the challenges, both inside and outside of the gym, there is a point when you need to recognize that it's time to seek help. Whether it be the mental toughness we needed to embody, the disregard for extreme levels of pain we were forced to embrace or the emotionlessness we ultimately fell into, perseverance sounds much better on paper. Couple this with goal-setting skills, which oftentimes in the gym resulted in plans to climb up the level ladder much quicker than is humanly possible. But what happens when perseverance is taken too far and you

---

18   Schultz, J., O'Reilly, J. and Cahn, SK. *Women and Sports in the United States.* Boston: Northeastern University Press. (2007).

19   "The Touchy Topic of Gymnasts and Body Weight, Eating Disorders and Nutrition (Part 1 of 4)." *Flogymnastics.Com.* (2013).

sacrifice your mental and physical well-being in order to achieve these higher-level skills?

* * *

My one-track mind was focused solely on improving my skills to advance levels. Outside the gym, this left me with no concept of what a non-gymnastics goal looked like. My whole life revolved around defining my success by what skills I was performing in the gym and how well I was performing them. While some things, like school, had come easy to me growing up, I could not identify one goal for my life that did not involve gymnastics in some capacity. Take gymnastics out of the picture and that left me with a huge gap to fill and a vulnerability for someone else to jump in and impose their definitions of success onto me.

"Less than 3% of all young girls will successfully compete in what USA Gymnastics considers the 'age group' program."[20]

All in all, this resulted in cycles of negativity in my life and a complete and utter denial of these negativities from me. At this point in my life I had experienced extreme pain for years, ignored it and continued to push on. Then, I had quite literally reached my breaking point, fracturing my back and being advised it was not wise to continue gymnastics and

20 Sharp, K. "Competitive Gymnastics for Young Girls: What to Expect." *Howtheyplay.* (2019).

nonetheless denied the fact that I had even injured myself in the first place. I had experienced unbearable levels of pain to the point where my body would no longer allow me to ignore it, and then unwillingly gave up the sport that I not only loved, but defined who I was as a person.

* * *

Samantha Peszek, a former Olympic gymnast, reminisced, "As much as I hate to admit it, I don't think you can ever truly 'retire' from the sport of gymnastics... it's just part of who you are... The things I'm proud of are those intangibles that I didn't know I was learning along the way... These are the things that are helping me in my life today. As hard as gymnastics can be, I'm so grateful that I was able to learn so much that has set me up for success in my life now (because) I STILL hate to make mistakes, but I sure as heck know how to pick myself back up and move on."[21]

* * *

I referred to myself as a gymnast above all else, and no longer being able to participate in the sport did not change this. This left me with a void to fill and a question I still had not yet answered: Is it true that all I would ever be is just a gymnast?

---

21   Peszek, S. Instagram Post. (2019).

CHAPTER 6

THINGS ARE NOT ALWAYS WHAT THEY SEEM

We were the picture-perfect couple. He'd meet me at my locker after class to walk me to my next one. I'd go to all of his baseball practices and games and sit on the bleachers to support him. We spent ample time together. We were the couple from the romantic comedy that everyone admired from afar, only none of this was truly indicative of what was really going on.

He met me at my locker because he wanted to be sure I wasn't interacting with anyone in a way he didn't approve of. I was at all of his practices and games because he threatened to hurt me if I wasn't. When we spent time together, he would spend hours explaining to me how worthless I was and how he was the only thing that would fill the void in my life that was created by not being able to do gymnastics anymore. He had convinced me that I had no identity without him, which was easy to do because at the time, I felt as though I had no identity without gymnastics.

But no one saw any of this. He was careful to only say and do these things in private. He threatened horrible things if I told my parents, or anyone for that matter. So, I continued to live in fear.

* * *

"This is what you deserve." Pinned against the wall I screamed for him not to touch me again and again. This only infuriated him more. I closed my eyes as tight as I could as I felt one hand firmly gripping my wrists and the other coming at my face. I squirmed trying to pull myself away. I failed. After all, he was way stronger than me, did I really expect to overpower him?

* * *

Friday night football. One of my favorite high school memories had sadly become one of my worst nightmares. My parents were away for the weekend and being an only child, I had the house to myself. I stood staring at myself in the mirror. I didn't recognize the reflection looking back at me. I brushed my hair into a ponytail, tightening my yellow cheerleading bow into just the right position.

* * *

"Smile, you can light up an entire room with your smile," my pop-pop's voice comforted me in my mind. I took a deep breath and forced the ends of my lips into an upward motion. *"Good enough,"* I thought to myself.

* * *

We got into the car silently. He reached for my hand across the center console. I pulled away. He maintained a steady, casual conversation for the entire fifteen-minute ride, which felt like fifteen hours at the time. I steadily nodded and murmured "yes" when appropriate. We pulled into the parking lot of our high school and I exited the car. "Don't tell a soul," he shot eyes at me, the same eyes that scared me into never opening my mouth to anyone about what was going on. I nodded passively and closed the door behind me. I was maintaining a steady grin, noticeable enough that people wouldn't question it, but not large enough for anyone to think I was having a great day.

* * *

The football game seemed to fly by that night in a dark haze. Before I knew it, I was walking back toward the parking lot. I ran into a girl I knew, my *best friend* at the time. I looked her dead in the eyes and I said, "I need help." She pushed it off and continued chatting about the boy she liked on the team who had played really well that night. I reached for her hand, "He hurt me. He hit me. He raped me." She rolled her eyes, "You're so dramatic, you're fine. Just go home, you have the whole house to yourselves tonight. You had to have sex eventually anyways."

My face grew white as I walked to his car. I got in. Maybe I was being dramatic. Maybe this was just "high school."

* * *

"Believe in new beginnings," my pop-pop's voice boomed in my head again. I wanted a new beginning. A beginning without this horrible monster I called my boyfriend. I shook it off, knowing my pop-pop would look over me.

* * *

We drove home in near silence. He inquired about the game, "We won." Pulling into my driveway he instantly unbuckled, ready to come inside.

"I'm tired. I'm going to bed." I retorted. "No, you're not. You're fine." He snapped at me. I ran into the house trying to close the door behind me before he could follow me inside. I failed. He barreled through the door, angry again.

* * *

"Deep breath, you are strong," the words boomed through my clouded mind. I could handle this.

* * *

After much physical struggle and verbal debate, I had finally removed him from my home. I locked the door behind me and peeked through the smoked glass, still nearly breathless from the fight. I ascended the stairs, wiping my eyes as tears still streamed down my face, silently crying in fear. I didn't sleep that night.

* * *

I lay staring at the ceiling, wishing I could hold my pop-pop's hand one more time. *"Believe in new beginnings."* I knew he was right; he always was. I hoped my new beginning was coming soon, without the monster.

* * *

After a year of dating, he had me fooled. This was *"love"* to me. This was *"normal"* to me. I thought I knew the man I called my boyfriend. But I didn't.

I had said no. I had told him to stop. But he still took advantage of me.

He was a monster. And he did not love me. And this was not love. And this was far from normal.

* * *

I debated telling my close friends, those forever friends. I debated telling my mom, my best friend. I debated telling anyone other than the *friend* who told me I was lying. The challenge was telling someone like them, someone real, meant this whole occurrence was real. Real, meaning something I was going to have to make sense of and talk about and most likely see someone about and maybe even be told I needed to report. I was sixteen and I wasn't ready for all of these realities.

* * *

And thus, I walked through the hallways and people stared at me. I kept to myself, head down, eyes watching the feet scurry past me. They treated me like I had some disease no one wanted to catch. They didn't think I heard the whispers calling me "dramatic" and "prude," but I heard them. Loud and clear. I felt the stares beaming at me and I swallowed hard.

* * *

I was the problem.

CHAPTER 7

I'M CURED! OH WAIT, THERE'S NO SUCH THING

———

Picture this: I am sixteen years old and just lost the love of my life. And no, I'm not referring to my monster of an ex-boyfriend; I'm referring to gymnastics. This newfound void is of newfound interest to a newfound boy. Not to mention, this newfound boy is part of the "cool" crowd. Intriguing, right?

Someone taking an interest in the "former gymnast" who has lost all sense of who she is. Someone taking interest in the struggling young girl newly navigating the social circles of high school as if it was her first day of her first year, yet she is three years in. Someone taking an interest in her innocence and her purity. Intriguing?

Or manipulative? Was this taking an interest or was this taking advantage of a vulnerable situation?

* * *

Remember, I am only sixteen so the red flags weren't waving quite as obviously as they are to you, or even as obviously as they do to me looking back on it now. The Monday morning quarterback always has all the answers. If only they could have given me a hint during the Friday night football game to run, and run as far and as fast as I could and never look back.

I had to be the problem, right? Who falls in (what I thought was) love with someone who was manipulating me?

Well, that's exactly it. The whole point was for me not to know that he had a plan. I was too close to the situation to truly know what was going on. And he knew that would be the case. But sixteen-year-old me was still convinced that I had somehow brought this upon myself. And he probably knew he had me convinced of this very thought.

* * *

I think by now you have probably noticed I am stubborn. I mean I fractured my back and yet I was convinced that no injury is bad enough to not finish a competition that I quite literally broke myself down even further. The void inside of me was so big that it legitimately took over my life. Gymnastics was everything I had and then I had nothing, or so I believed at the time.

Worthlessness was booming through the void that filled my body. When a boy swooped in and convinced me I was valuable, making me feel the slightest bit of worth again, he filled a small part of that void. Insert a full year of buildup and manipulation and you can see how I had a false sense of fulfillment and he had me wrapped around his finger like a puppet.

Worthlessness is often underestimated until you feel it for yourself. Sure enough, he took advantage of my vulnerability because, let's be honest, love even when it's not real love, is vulnerable.

Now add in the fact that I had attempted to speak my vulnerability to someone I thought I could trust and she denied me; not only denied me, but disregarded my words entirely. She took my vulnerability and tore it apart. When you tell someone something and they don't believe you, it sucks. When you tell someone something important and they don't believe you, it sucks even more. When you tell someone something that is so intimately vulnerable and personal and they don't believe you, well, you get the point.

* * *

Senior year of high school and I was only sixteen, so naturally, I thought I had it all figured out. I had told myself that as long as I got rid of those two, toxic people in my life, I would be fine. Rather than reaching out to those I could absolutely trust, like my mom and my forever friends, I retreated deeper into a false sense of "cured." After all, I was resilient. There was no stopping me. I got admitted to the school of my dreams: The University of Michigan. I would officially be spending the next four years in Ann Arbor—as far away from those horrible people as I could get. Life was all good again, or so I had convinced myself.

I think back now and wish I could hug sixteen-year-old me and tell her she doesn't have to do this all on her own. As you recall, I am very close with my mom, but I didn't want to tell her about what had happened, or more importantly, how I was feeling because I didn't want even the slightest chance that she would blame herself for not recognizing the monsters that were surrounding me. Clearly, they hid it well or at least I would have noticed, being so close to both of them for a full year.

Instead of employing a support and empowerment team, I turned inward and resorted to denial. Does that sound familiar? It should because I am famous for denying the things I don't want to deal with.

You can start to see a pattern forming here: deny that I am in pain, deny the injury, deny the fact that I can no longer be a gymnast, deny that I am no longer a gymnast, deny that I am feeling a strong loss of identity, deny that I was taken advantage of, deny that she hadn't believed me.

* * *

Denial is more common in all of us than we would like to believe. A lot of the time we feel like we are better off denying that we are struggling than facing the problem head on. It seems easier, simpler, and more straightforward. And it is, in the moment anyway. This catches up to us later down the line when that one simple thing we denied has now snowballed into a very large problem and we have a complete breakdown or blowout, depending on how exactly things get to us.

Personally, I have a breakdown.

CHAPTER 8

WHAT IS LOVE?

———

I want to take a minute here to discuss exactly what love is, to me anyway. I have used the word a lot throughout this book so far and I feel the need to step back and discover exactly what I mean when I use that word.

* * *

Let's start with my love for the sport of gymnastics. This love is indicative of fulfillment. It offered me a feeling of completeness and fueled an excitement within me that was, and still is in some ways, unmatched.

Then there is what I thought was love for my ex-boyfriend. This love was manipulative and abused power. He had been in a position of power due to my vulnerability at the time and he intuitively manipulated me into believing I needed him.

There is the love for my forever friends. This love is authentic. They love me for who I am and I love them for who they are. We embrace each other's uniqueness and further each other's spontaneity.

Lastly, the love for my family, specifically my mom, is twofold. It is innate, but also treasurable. It is fruitful, encouraging, and supportive. It is invaluable. It fuels my everyday inspiration to empower myself and empower others. It is believing in me even on the toughest days. It is truly forever.

* * *

As you can see love is many things. But love should never hurt. Love should never make you feel less than you are. Love should never tear you down. Love is not easy, but love should always be beautiful.

* * *

"Being deeply loved by someone gives you strength, while loving someone deeply gives you courage."[22]

---

22 Lao Tzu.

CHAPTER 9

YOU DON'T ALWAYS HAVE TO FIT IN

Going into college I had not told a soul about that night.

No one, other than that girl that used to be my best friend, knew. I couldn't tell my parents for they might have blamed themselves and I couldn't tell my friends for they might not have believed me. I avoided relationships at all costs. I continued believing I was the problem. I joined a sorority, whose philanthropy was domestic violence, with the thought that maybe, one day, I would gather the courage to share my story.

* * *

Fraternity parties deepened my fear. A dark room filled with a ton of drunk men in the comfort of their own home; I felt vulnerable. Soon I would have to realize that not all men were like this; however, this only lessened my fear. It did not solve the underlying anxiety I felt building inside of me that was weighing on my chest every day, making it hard to breathe.

At the time, I so badly wanted to believe I was over it. He was a thing of my past and I would never subject myself to a relationship like that again. Everyone around me seemed to be living their lives so free-spirited. No one else shuddered every time someone stood behind them or took a step too close. No one else cautiously and meticulously picked out clothing that would cover the most skin possible, even on the hottest days. No one else brought only their own drinks to parties, fearful that someone might slip something into it. No one else lived in constant and all-encompassing fear.

I found myself falling deeper and deeper into the trap of an incessant need to *fit in*. I started changing the way I dressed and found a newfound interest in drinking that I never had in the past. I had plenty of *friends*, if you could call them that. Only one of them really knew me, and she was my roommate and she didn't belong to the new Greek Life social circle I was trying to conform to.

I felt *"cool"* because I was being validated through Instagram likes and Facebook event invites. This became my new measure of friendship and I watched myself slowly slip away until I did not even recognize the girl in the mirror.

I found myself engaging in social events I would have never found appealing. The people did not share the same values that I did. The parties were far too often and far too dark. The drinking was excessive and to the point of sickness. The culture was too giving of your body without any regard for who the person really was.

Through succumbing to peer influence, I accepted an invitation from a boy I was not entirely close with to a formal date party out of town. I thought of how fun this would be and reminded myself there were going to be other people there that I knew. I told myself that it would be exciting to see a new place and meet new people.

* * *

The weekend started off great. We explored the city and we shared great meals. We shared a hotel room with another couple, which *definitely* would keep me safe from him taking advantage of me because other people were around.

We got dressed for the club we would be attending that night for the formal date party. I blew out my hair, put on my makeup, and dressed for the event. I was excited. It would be fun. I was branching out, but most of all, I was *fitting in*.

A few more couples came into our room to hang out prior to leaving for the club. My date had made a few drinks for everyone in the room and handed me one. Losing control of a situation is my biggest fear, so I sipped slowly so as not to get too intoxicated.

The music blared and suddenly, the night went dark.

* * *

The next thing I remember is waking up the following morning. I was alarmed. How could this have happened? I had one drink.

I looked down and realized I had nothing on, but an unfamiliar t-shirt. I looked to my left and my date lay beside me still asleep. I looked to my right and the couple we shared a room with was also still asleep. The other girl was a *friend* of mine.

I woke her gently. I asked her to come to the bathroom with me. I asked her what had happened the night before. She looked at me confused.

"There's no way you were drugged. You're being dramatic. Are you just embarrassed you had sex with him? It's not a big deal. Sex is normal. Go back to bed." The words pierced like a knife.

* * *

My face grew white. Maybe I hadn't found my new beginning. I turned internally again, denying that the weekend ever even occurred. I never spoke of it again.

* * *

Just a few weeks later the same boy that had taken advantage of me, sexually assaulted my friend.

She texted me, not knowing of my past experience with him, informing me of the situation. I comforted her as she cried and explained to her that though this was not easy, she would get through it. I told her how she was a warrior and she deserved respect and love, not this awful behavior. I told her not to live in fear, for things would get better in time. I told her I would be here for her, to listen or talk, whichever she needed. I told her I would help her seek professional help if that is what she wanted. I hugged her as she cried.

I was telling her all of the things I needed to hear myself.

* * *

As I ventured home from her place, I fished my phone out of my pocket. I dialed my mom's phone number, but I couldn't get myself to hit call. I opened my messages in my "Phoenix Foxes" group chat. I moved my thumbs slowly over the letters, hovering, but not clicking. How exactly do I begin this text? "I got raped." No, too harsh. "I *think* I got raped." No, I didn't *think,* I knew. I closed my messages app and slipped my phone back into my pocket. There was no right way to say this, and, therefore, it felt as though there was no way to say it at all.

* * *

I walked into my bedroom and it finally hit me that this was real. He was a rapist. He was no different than my ex-boyfriend who had assaulted me. I couldn't breathe. I couldn't speak. I couldn't move. I laid there for days, silent and paralyzed.

* * *

I was the problem.

CHAPTER 10

THE BUMP IN THE ROAD
I NEVER SAW COMING

—

I swore off the fraternity life. It had to have been the environment I was encompassed by that caused the problem. I stayed
away from those people who engaged in an unnecessary
amount of partying and I immersed myself in various other
outlets at school. I gave up the need to fit in. I was *maturing*.

I was in full control of myself and I would never let someone
make me feel powerless again. If I was ever faced with this
same sense of stolen agency, I would surely be able to tackle it
seamlessly. I was in charge of my own life and I would make
everyone who came in contact with me know that.

* * *

One outlet I had immersed myself in was a professional growth office through the college I was a part of within Michigan, which connects you with school alumni to learn from their experiences and network within the professional world. I had been selected to introduce the Dean of the College of Literature, Arts, and Science at a professional event.

I met a boy there. He was kind. He was intelligent. He was respectful. But that was always people's first impression. I didn't believe in first impressions anymore.

He asked me on a date. I accepted, hesitantly, and expected to find the one thing wrong with him that I could obsess over, amplify, and then justify why I had a wall up that I would not let anyone break through.

I didn't. There was nothing to obsess over. He was kind. He was intelligent. He was respectful. I never liked anyone anymore, I didn't let myself. But I liked him a little. We spent time together. We got to know one another. He was still kind. He was still intelligent. He was still respectful.

There always seems to be expectations at this age. Those were my fear.

* * *

I struggled to get the words out. "Things have to be on my timeline," I said. "I have to be comfortable," I said. "It's okay if that's not okay with you." I quickly uttered, knowing it wasn't actually okay. I started apologizing incessantly as if I was wrong for taking ownership of my own body and the choices I made with my own body.

"I want you to be comfortable, so you have the reigns," he said. I smiled. I got a single breath in. That was more than I had ever gotten in. It was *progress*. It was *coping*. It was *overcoming*.

* * *

Later in the month he asked me to his formal date party. A weekend out of town. "It is on your timeline, there are no expectations." He told me.

But apparently it wasn't him I needed to worry about.

* * *

We went to a brunch with bottomless mimosas and by the end of the event, my date was nowhere to be found. *I knew my timeline would not be good enough for him*, I thought to myself. *I should not have come.*

* * *

I headed back to the hotel with the other couple we shared a room with. The girl had left the room to go get ice and I went into the bathroom to wash up. Her date pushed into the bathroom and shoved me against the wall. My chest collapsed into itself as the flashbacks poured back into my mind. I tried to drown out what he was doing in the moment.

"Stop. I am not interested. Please stop. No."

He slid his free hand over my mouth uttering aggressively, "Do not tell a soul I swear to God." We heard his date opening the door to the room a few minutes later and he pulled away and pushed out of the bathroom. I remained against the wall, tears streaming down my face quietly.

* * *

When we got back home the next day, I decided to tell some friends. They had me talk to him about it. I texted him, telling him how disgusting and disappointing his actions were, especially since I had known him since my freshman year of college and I thought he was a *friend*. He was confused and claimed to not remember. He told me he was drugged and he did not mean to hurt me.

My friends told me to have him come over to apologize. We sat around my dining room table as I watched him look like the victim. Everyone sat there staring at me as he apologized and blamed his actions on the drugs.

The staring felt all too familiar.

* * *

I only ever saw my date from that weekend when we would occasionally pass one another on campus. I never looked up, never smiled, never waved, for I could never forgive him for deciding my timeline wasn't good enough for him.

I've never confirmed if he knows what his friend did to me, but I'm sure he has heard rumors. He never reached out, never checked in with me. Turns out he wasn't kind, intelligent, or respectful.

* * *

This time felt different. It seemed to bring me quite close to my breaking point. I was starting to recognize just how toxic the people I was surrounding myself with were. I had been brainwashed into trusting people and thinking they would always have my back. I was almost too privileged in having my forever friends. It made me believe, far too easily, that all friends would be just as reliable as they are. While most of these toxic people may have had good intentions, none of them were prioritizing my well-being.

It was time to open up to those closest and most trusted in my life: my mom and my forever friends. This was not going to be easy, but I had finally recognized the necessity of talking these things into reality by opening up to those who would fight these challenges alongside me.

I spent the next three days in bed at what felt lower than rock bottom. Everyone kept telling me how "sorry he was" and how he "wasn't even eating because he was sick over this whole thing."

I had said no. I had told him to stop. But he still took advantage of me.

What they seemed to forget was how I was feeling.

* * *

I still somehow felt like I was the problem.

PART TWO

LOOKING DEEPER

CHAPTER 11

HOW A MANIPULATIVE DOCTOR AND AN INSPIRING PATIENT HELPED ME SHARE MY STORY

———

"Breaking News: Nassar faces sexual assault allegations, fired by MSU."

There were 332 young women sexually assaulted by Larry Nassar.

There were 332 young women who were made to believe they were the problem.

It took twenty-two years to finally have someone believe them.

After twenty-two years of abuse, he was sentenced to 125 years in prison.

Finally, Judge Rosemarie Aquilina declared that, in fact, he was the problem.

There was no breaking news telling my story.

There was one young woman who was sexually assaulted.

There was one young woman who was made to believe she was the problem.

It took nineteen years to finally have someone believe her.

After three years, she came to love herself again.

Finally, she declared that, in fact, they were the problem.

At twenty-three, Aly spoke of how she was fifteen when she was first sexually assaulted. I listened to her in countless interviews, speaking on how she was still processing and coping with that fact.

At nineteen, I spoke of how I was sixteen when I was first sexually assaulted. I stood up and told my story to my close family members and friends about how I was still processing and coping with that fact.

Aly did the Sports Illustrated Swimsuit photoshoot. She embraced her body and expressed her love for herself. She spoke about how while it is hard to talk about the tough times in life, they are just as essential as the good times in shaping who we are.

I joined SHEI Magazine, a student-run fashion, arts, and culture magazine at the University of Michigan. I embraced my creative expression through clothing and this further developed my confidence in myself. I began to distance myself from the negativity in my life, but I did not try to rid myself of it completely. Rather, I immersed myself in positivity in my life, allowing the negativity to be a counteractive symbol of positivity.

Aly struggled with the media trying to define her as only a victim of sexual assault. The media questioned why she did not speak up sooner. She spoke out against victim shaming and helped facilitate the shift of power to the survivors.

I struggled with being outspoken, hoping people would not define me as a victim. People I thought were *friends* asked me why I did not speak up sooner. I took a stand for myself and owned my past, no longer allowing others to diminish my experiences. I continued to speak up throughout the struggle with the hope that my story and my small form of activism may help other survivors, even if it was just one individual, to not feel alone. I am a survivor.

Aly spoke at the 2018 Espys, empowering survivors to speak their truths and offering them sisterhood.

I spoke in my classes and my extracurricular groups telling others to speak their truths and offering them a friend. I recognized that people around me may be struggling and I did not want them to feel as though they were alone.

Aly released the "In Her Own Words" project with Sports Illustrated and spoke about how she hopes no one ever has to feel ashamed about what they have been through and that the next generation should not have to say the words "me too."

I got my lotus flower tattoo. A beautiful flower growing in muddy water, a true testament to something beautiful coming of something ugly.

Our stories may not be perfectly aligned, but Aly Raisman's words echo through my head to this day. Hearing her words of empowerment and of faith in a greater good brought me to a better place; her words brought me to a stronger place. I told my mom, I sought out professional help, and I got my lotus flower tattoo to be my gentle reminder on the hard days. Now came the next step: coming to terms with my feelings and eventually navigating therapy, which I like to call the never-ending maze.

But first, a word with an anonymous Nassar survivor on being a warrior.

CHAPTER 12

THERE IS PLENTY OF LIGHT STILL LEFT TO SPREAD

———

I had the pleasure of speaking with a very inspiring individual who has chosen to remain anonymous at this time. She is a Nassar survivor. She interacted with him on less of a grand stage than the Olympics, but rather a space that is supposed to be safe, her home gym.

I happen to be very friendly with a teammate of hers, who recommended I speak to her as she is such an empowering individual. Walking into the interview, I had expected to hear a heart-wrenching story of a young child who was broken by a trusted professional. I expected to hear of immense struggle and pain. I expected to hear of dark times that have since been brightened by lighter times. Knowing every story is very different, I had not expected to hear parts of my young self in her young self.

We have not had the same experiences. Yet, we shared similar tones in how we described the darker times, and similarly, yet contrastingly, the lighter times.

* * *

This young woman spoke words of optimism that, quite literally, shed light on my day. She spoke of her strong familial foundation that helped her to recognize, and remain in touch with, the reality that there was much more to her than just a gymnast at a very young age. "The culture of gymnastics promotes silencing and emotionlessness," she regretfully uttered. She spoke of how she regrets to have given into those damaging realities.

As a sophomore in college, she realized that she needed an emotional and mental outlet where she could engage in wellness and healthfulness as she was feeling quite down internally at the time. She found this outlet in yoga, which she still does regularly today. In 2019, the National Institute for the Clinical Application of Behavioral Medicine explored the question of whether yoga could heal patient trauma, specifically those who were sexually assaulted, "what they found was surprising. The patients who attended the weekly yoga group, with its guided meditation and breathing exercises, were much better able to focus on the present moment and control their impulses."[23] This is so important for a survivor in the process of coping because it can help them accept their past for what it was and use what it taught them about strength and resilience to further their bravery and confidence in the future.

Ultimately, she is extremely grateful that she had this outlet in yoga when the Nassar trial began, as she feels her life was transformed for the better before her true realization of the damage had started. This foundational wellness allowed her to begin the healing process before consciously understanding how dark and scary this road would be. While she recognizes that she is not fully healed, she is hopeful that she is healing herself by slowly peeling back the layers of damage, some layers she did not even realize were there to begin with.

* * *

She exceeded my expectations in more than just straightforward ways. She allowed me to further reflect on my own experiences in a whole new light. She allowed me to feel more

---

23 "Could Yoga Hold the Key to Healing a Patient's Trauma?" *NICABM*. (2019).

at peace with the fact that this is a journey that we must take day by day, or better yet, "layer by layer." I was blown away by her honesty and fragility, that exuded confidence and empowerment. I am honored to have gotten to interview her, and I am pleased to have her as a peer, and even as a friend, to share my experiences with.

* * *

Finally, she spoke of the future by saying that doing bad does not solve bad, and she hopes to see positive changes in the gymnastics world culture. She commenced, "We are warriors, everyday fighting to be the best person we can be."

* * *

My number one supporter who has helped me fight every single day to be the best person I can be is definitely my mom. I could not be the warrior I am today without her by my side, and, thus, I have explored the journey of letting her in on my dark realities.

CHAPTER 13

I'M MORE ME WHEN I'M WITH YOU

—

My mom is my best friend. Hands down, no questions asked. This made it extremely difficult to tell her I was struggling. I worried she would internalize it and wish she would have done more or asked more questions at the time it was happening. I worried she would want to legally report it to the police and I did not want to go that route; I had relived those day enough times, I did not want to do it in court too. I worried most of all though, that telling her would make it all a reality. Which is why I waited.

And waited, and waited, and waited.

* * *

Sometimes, the people closest to us are the hardest to tell. Once we tell them, it becomes reality. It becomes a part of our every day life. It becomes something we have to confront.

But it also becomes something we begin to cope with. Something we begin to tackle. Something we begin to overcome. And most of all, something we can fight.

* * *

There were countless times I almost told her. Numerous moments where her number was dialed, but I just couldn't get myself to click call. More even when I would begin a sentence, quickly followed by me changing the subject because I had cowered thinking about what emotions might be brought up by telling her.

When I finally did tell her, she was so loving and so supportive it made me question why I worried for all of that time. After all, she made every obstacle in life easier to tackle. She has been my guiding light since the day I was born and has never guided me wrong.

She has always instilled confidence in me, assuring me that "what's for you shall not pass you."

It was hard to have the most important person in my life hearing the absolute worst thing that I have ever experienced, but by letting her into my darkness she was able to act as my light. Sure enough, she has helped me cope and fight like no other. She has helped me redefine what it means to be a warrior. In fact, I would never be in as good of a place as I am today without her, for more reasons than just this.

* * *

I always joke with my mom that me no longer being a gymnast was the best thing that happened to our relationship. While this is true in some small and insignificant capacity, I mostly say it to poke fun at her. My mom is my number one fan, but with gymnastics, she was also my number one critic. As I mentioned earlier, she wanted to be a gymnast her whole young life. She also owns a gymnastics facility. She has been encompassed in the sport just as long as I have, if not longer. This means she has developed an appreciation for the sport that sprouted a passion within her extremely similar to my passion. She was never negative in any way, rather she just saw the potential and talent I had inside of me and she wanted me to succeed more than I could fathom.

When I first got hurt, it seemed as though she panicked. She had never seen me in such raw and crushing pain. The look on her face read, "I would take all of the pain on myself if it meant you didn't have to suffer." That's my mom.

She is selfless. She is always giving of herself and rarely getting the same in return from those she gives to.

It is admirable, but it also makes me sad sometimes. That's why I do my best to show my appreciation for her at all times because she truly is a blessing.

* * *

She has taught me to be resilient, inspiring me through more than just her words, but also her actions. She takes on new challenges with grace and conquers them seamlessly and has taught me to do just the same.

She is constantly assuring me, "the best is yet to come."

The countless number of times my mom has believed in me when I couldn't believe in myself is just one thing that I am incredibly grateful for. There are not enough words of appreciation in this world for how deeply and truly I appreciate my mom.

After all, simply put, "I'm more me when I'm with you."

CHAPTER 14

FOR THOSE STILL WONDERING... WHY I DIDN'T REPORT

This is a hard topic to cover.

* * *

I'm not completely sure why I never reported. By the time I had come to terms with the reality of what had happened, it had been a pretty long time that had passed, as you all know through reading about my journey up until this point.

You also have to recognize my frame of mind when it originally happened: I was petrified. I didn't want to draw any extra attention to myself; I wanted to hide. I didn't want to tell more people; the people I had told claimed I was lying.

If the circumstances were different, I can't say what I would have done. Maybe I would have handled things differently, but all things considered, this was the decision I made at that time.

* * *

Legally speaking, I should have reported it.

Every single one of those men deserve to serve the consequences for their actions. I know that for a fact. However, when it comes to sexual assault, the legal system is tricky. I could talk about the legal system surrounding this issue for a long time, but I am not an expert.

One fact I do know to be true is that, "nearly eighty percent of rapes and sexual assaults go unreported, according to a Justice Department analysis of violent crime in 2016."[24]

I'm not sure what would have come of it if I had pursued any of these cases legally. I do know, however, that it would

---

24 Kimble, C. and Chettiar, IM. "Sexual Assault Remains Dramatically Under-Reported | Brennan Center for Justice." *Brennancenter.Org.* (2018).

have been hard to prove. The first time it was my boyfriend, the second time drugs were involved, and the third we were alone. There were no witnesses, no one backing up my story.

After all, out of every 1,000 sexual assaults, 995 perpetrators walk free.[25]

The bottom line is I was just a young female out in the world on her own, hiding out of the shame that these manipulative people had brought upon me.

* * *

Something also to note is this recurring and debilitating feeling that I was the problem. Due to the intense manipulation I had been subjected to and the constant convincing that I was not a valuable human being, I was conditioned to believe I was the problem. While there was a little part of me that would fight back at that thought, ultimately the environment I was trapped in kept winning the battle. I was a young female who was not fully ready to take agency over my life.

And thus, I continued to believe I was the problem.

* * *

---

25   "The Criminal Justice System: Statistics | RAINN." *Rainn.Org.* (2019).

"99% of rapists get away with it."

"1 in 5 women will be sexually assaulted at some point during their college career in the United States."

"Less than 10% will ever report their assault to the school or to the police. Those who do, usually wait about 11 months before they report."

"90% of sexual assaults are committed by repeat offenders."

"Only 6% of sexual assaults reported to the police end with the assailant spending a single day in prison."[26]

Now, also recognize the fact that most of the time the reason they get away with it is because the survivor feels like no one will believe them. Essentially, they feel alone in their battle.

* * *

So, what is the solution?

"What these women (who don't report) wish they'd had in college is pretty simple; they wanted a website, one they could use at the time and place that felt safest to them with clearly

---

26 Ladd, J. "The Reporting System That Sexual Assault Survivors Want." Presentation, TED. (2016).

written information about their reporting options, with the ability to electronically report their assault, rather than having the first step to go in and talk to someone who may or may not believe them. With the option to create a secure, timestamped document of what happened to them, preserving evidence even if they don't want to report yet. And lastly, and perhaps most critically, with the ability to report their assault only if someone else reported the same assailant. You see, knowing that you weren't the only one changes everything. It changes the way you frame your own experience; it changes the way you think about your perpetrator, it means that if you do come forward, you'll have someone else's back and they'll have yours.

And we included a unique matching system where if (the assailant's) first victim had come forward, saved her record, entered into the matching system and named (the assailant), and (the assailant's) second victim had done the same thing a few months later, they would have matched and the verified contact information of both survivors would have been sent to the authorities at the same time for investigation and follow up.

We could prevent 59 percent of sexual assaults just by stopping repeat perpetrators earlier on. And because we're creating a real deterrent to assault, for perhaps the first time, maybe (the assailants') of the world would never even try to assault anyone.

The type of system I'm describing, the type of system that survivors want is a type of information escrow, meaning an entity that holds on to information for you and only releases it to a third party when certain pre-agreed upon conditions are met, such as a match. The application that we built is for college campuses. But the same type of system could be used in the military or even the workplace...

We don't have to live in a world where 99 percent of rapists get away with it. We can create one where those who do wrong are held accountable, where survivors get the support and justice they deserve, where the authorities get the information they need, and where there's a real deterrent to violating the rights of another human being."[27]

A true solution would be for no one to ever be sexually assaulted or abused ever again. But unfortunately, some people are evil and righteous and we live amongst them. Jessica Ladd's system of pairing and reporting, however, does minimize the risk of these evil beings striking again and, therefore, it is a step forward in minimizing the immense number of traumatic events occurring every day. I strive to live in a world where no survivor ever has to feel alone.

* * *

---

27 Ladd, J. "The Reporting System That Sexual Assault Survivors Want." Presentation, TED. (2016).

A system such as this would have been beneficial to me following my second assault. If you recall, after leaving my friend's house who told me she had also been assaulted by the same man who drugged and assaulted me, that is when the fact began to sink in that that man, as well as, my ex-boyfriend were rapists. I had felt so alone that my mind had conditioned itself to believe I was the problem. I can't say if this system would have put those men in jail; I can't say if this system would have prevented my third sexual assault; but I can say, with full confidence, that this system would have reassured me that I was not the problem and I was not alone. In fact, this system would have allowed me to begin my healing process long before my healing process began in reality.

* * *

Clearly this was not an ideal situation. I still wonder if I did the right thing letting these people walk around without ever having been reprimanded legally for their actions. I have considered pursuing the cases now, but I just don't know that it would make me feel any better about it. I have closed those doors and opened tons of new ones. Whether this is the right mindset to have, I'm not sure. All I do know for sure is that these were my experiences and I chose how I wanted to handle them on my own, knowing full well now that I was not responsible for these occurrences and thus, I was never the problem.

So right, wrong, or indifferent, respecting my decision is very important. Mostly because it is the system of justice surrounding this topic that kept me from making another decision at the time, but also because I feel empowered by the fact that I was able to make this choice for and by myself.

A LETTER FROM MY SECOND MOM, DANI:
NO ONE SHOULD HAVE TO SUFFER IN SILENCE

As a former Special Agent with the FBI for twenty-four years, most of my career was spent investigating violent crimes. For fourteen years, I was the primary investigator for Child Exploitation cases. All of the victims in my cases were children who had been sexually abused by adults and exploited online.

Due to this experience, I often spoke to my daughter and her gymnastics teammates, including Serena, about online safety and ways to protect themselves from such predators. Many of the victims in my cases sought attention from strangers online because they had a poor self-image, desperately were longing for attention, or were extremely vulnerable due to an unstable family environment, all resulting in feelings that no one in the world cared about them.

* * *

I will never forget the day Serena disclosed what had happened to her. I was shocked, angry, upset, but most of all, I felt like I had failed her. Serena, my daughter from another mother, had been raped. She had been in an abusive relationship and I, the investigator, never had a clue.

She didn't fit the victim profile I was all too familiar with.

* * *

I should have spoken to her, my daughter, and the other girls about what healthy relationships look and feel like and the warning signs of unhealthy ones. I should have spoken to them about off-line predators and how to handle them. I should have spoken to them about self-defense and what to do if they felt their physical safety was at risk. But most importantly, I should have spoken to them about never being afraid to tell someone that you have been sexually abused.

No one should have to suffer in silence and have their life be defined by trauma and pain.

* * *

To my Serena, I am sorry that I never spoke to you about these things.

Nonetheless, I am so very proud of how you did not let these difficult events in your life define who you are. Your courage and bravery in sharing your story with the world will help others who have experienced abuse and will inspire parents to have these difficult, but extremely important, conversations with their children so they do not become future victims.

CHAPTER 15

THE JAGGED PATH OF COPING AND HEALING IN THE WIDE WORLD OF THERAPY

———

Therapy is weird.

That's not to say I am against it, because I look forward to seeing (or now talking on the phone with) Jen once a week (even when she tells me things I may not want to hear).

Therapy is weird because the process of finding the right therapist for you is difficult.

* * *

I am now eighteen and have finally come to terms with the
fact that I have, in fact, been sexually assaulted by three different men. Now I have to get up the courage to tell my mom.
I need to figure out how exactly to go about doing that in the
first place. I need to find a therapist. Mind you, I still need to
process this whole situation myself. I am still suffering from
intense feelings of worthlessness that I am partially denying
just so I can get through another day.

So, I repeat: therapy is weird.

The process begins with you searching the internet for the
best rated therapist. Then you read a bunch of reviews from
their patients. Look through photos of them. Read about
their degrees and their specialty. It's legitimately a form
of stalking. It's weird. And I haven't even gotten to the
weirdest part. You do all of this just to end up face to face
with a complete and total stranger that you are expecting
to somehow "heal" you.

So, I affirm: therapy is definitely weird.

The thing is though, once you find the right therapist, it isn't
weird. In fact, it is wonderful.

But that's not to say that finding the right one was an easy task because it was anything but easy.

* * *

First, I saw the "sexual assault specialist."

This woman sat across from me asking questions with a judgmental "what happened in your childhood to cause this" look on her face. I told her about suffering from what I assumed to be anxiety attacks and how the only time I felt like I could fully breathe is when I was talking to my mom. So naturally, she tried to convince me that I was not self-aware and my relationship with my mom was unhealthy. Which completely turned me off since my mom is the only thing that relieved my anxiety and I had taken it upon myself to seek out help since I knew I was off balance. Let's just say I did not leave that office very happy. I stood up abruptly, declaring that no one would speak about my mother that way and that she had no business telling me whether I was self-aware or not after knowing me for a total of two hours and fifteen minutes. So, after two and one-fourth sessions, I left and never returned. Most important to note, no one messes with my mom.

Strike one.

* * *

Then there was the psychiatrist.

I sat down and she said abruptly, "tell me what is wrong with you." I proceeded to start explaining the story of my first sexual assault to which she cut me off declaring she "did not have enough time to hear everything so make it quick." Naturally, this irritated me, but I continued nonetheless only to be cut-off again ten minutes later. She had determined I was suffering from "social anxiety and generalized depression." Let's keep in mind, I did not say I was sad in any way, shape, or form. I actually described how I had such a strong support team of friends and family (you know who you are). I was not only not sad, but I was overwhelmingly grateful for all of the support I had. She closed the session by telling me it would take about two months to place me with a psychologist since my case was not classified as "urgent," but she could prescribe me something for depression in the meantime. I obviously declined the pills that she had no business prescribing me in the first place after knowing me for a total of fifteen minutes and left the office. I dodged the call from the office two months later when they finally decided it was "urgent" enough to get around to helping me.

Strike two.

* * *

With two strikes in the book, my mom suggested looking into online therapy.

She said maybe I would have better luck if I wasn't sitting face to face from the person as it would feel like less pressure. I signed up for online therapy sessions. At first, it was actually pretty good. The woman was sweet and she had suggested some pretty standard, but still useful, coping mechanisms. Then one day I logged into my portal and my therapist had changed. The only explanation: my old one no longer felt she could help me. Feeling very blatantly rejected, I cancelled my subscription.

Strike three.

* * *

I spent months boycotting the idea of therapy, convinced no one could help me but myself. Ignorant, I know. My mom was supportive, but I could tell she was worried. She knew I needed to talk to someone and that someone could not be her, but she also didn't want to force me into it. A couple of months into my pity party, my friend suggested a new therapist to me. He had been seeing this therapist himself for separate reasons, but he thought that maybe she could help me too. He gently described her to me, highlighting the fact that she, too, had been sexually assaulted. "Maybe she will be able to better understand what you are feeling since she went through it herself. I know every case is different, but I think it's worth the try." I was reluctant, but I had accepted the fact that I could not do this on my own anymore.

This is how I found Jen!

* * *

Therapy takes a certain level of trust, not only in your therapist and their capabilities to help you cope and heal, but also in yourself to stay true to your emotions. This is easier said than done and, oftentimes, is the main reason why therapy might be failing you. It is extremely difficult to admit to yourself that what you are feeling is justified, especially when others are denying you that justification. It is even more difficult to then speak this truth about your feelings into a reality by sharing them with your therapist. Trusting is essential in the process of therapy, but even more essential is wanting to help yourself.

You need to want to cope; you need to want to heal; you need to want to share, no matter how hard that can be at times.

* * *

I am not going to explicitly detail how our sessions go because that is between us, but let me assure you that when you find the right therapist it is definitely not weird.

It is very emotional.

It is exhausting at times.

It is always empowering.

It is constantly inspiring.

But most of all, it is very far from weird. In fact, it is wonderful.

CHAPTER 16

WHY THE WORDS "I'M SORRY" ARE MY WORST NIGHTMARE

———

I realize calling the words "I'm sorry" my worst nightmare seems extreme. I want to recognize the fact that I know people have good intentions when they say I'm sorry.

* * *

Here is my qualm: imagine being in the shoes of a survivor, or in the words of my very strong friend we heard from earlier, a warrior.

They feel you have provided them with a safe enough space to share. They get up the courage to tell you their story, and you respond with, "I'm sorry." The natural response to "I'm sorry" is typically "it's okay." I think we all can agree, it most definitely was not okay that this happened to me, or to any of the other women and men this has happened to. In reality, you cannot be sorry for the experiences that we have undergone because you did not make those experiences happen. So, while I appreciate the intended gesture, I urge you to try to refrain from saying those words.

* * *

Now you may be thinking, what is a better response?

Just simple reassurance and encouragement is effective. Acknowledging the person's worth and offering support is definitely the most effective, in my opinion. If that is all you are comfortable with contributing, that's fine because not much more is necessary. Of course, there are situations with those you are closer to and those conversations will be far more extensive, but this is generally applicable for those you do not know as intimately.

I also recognize that every person is different and this is not a clear-cut response guide for every person you will encounter who has undergone these experiences. I think it is important to read the situation on a case-by-case basis and offer support if nothing else. No one can ever have too much support.

CHAPTER 17

WE'VE ONLY JUST SCRATCHED THE SURFACE

———

I've used a lot of loaded language throughout my book journey so far... but what do I really mean when I use words such as "anxiety" or "body image" or "mental health" or even "survivor"?

I could get very technical here, however, if you can't tell by this point, I am not a "by the book" type of person. There is a lot more lying beneath the surface than the simple definitions of these words.

In fact, there is nothing simple about these words and their meanings at all.

Anxiety is increasingly more common in our everyday conversations. A simple Google search will tell you anxiety is "a feeling of worry, nervousness, or unease, typically about an imminent event or something with an uncertain outcome."[28] The psychological system then decides that if your feelings of anxiety are not defined by this simple definition, then your feelings are not justified. Anxiety, which is experienced differently by every single person, can't be condensed into one straightforward sentence.

The thing is, in actuality, Google spit back "about 415,000,000 results" for just this one word alone. That seems way more accurate than just that one sentence. There are countless people who suffer from anxiety, some cases are mild and others are completely debilitating. There is post-traumatic stress disorder anxiety, social anxiety, situational anxiety, public speaking anxiety, generalized anxiety, obsessive compulsive disorder anxiety, specific phobia-related anxiety, panic disorder anxiety, and this list does not even begin to cover all of the cases. To classify all of these cases with the same one sentence is wildly unfair and extremely inaccurate.

---

28 Definition of anxiety. *Dictionary.Com*. (2019).

Similarly, not everyone can use the same coping mechanisms or resources to aid them in their healing process. Personally, I am extremely grateful to have my therapist, Jen, as well as my mom, and my close friends to confide in, but these resources are not the solution for everyone.

Whenever I tell people I have anxiety they seem to think I am lying. I generally come off as a confident and put together person, so no one would assume I suffer from anxiousness on the interior as I do not show it on the exterior. While it did take time to get my anxiety under control enough that I do not show signs of it on the exterior, it doesn't mean my anxiety is cured completely on the interior. The thing with mental health disorders, such as anxiety, is there is no "right" way to be. Just because I may present better in front of a crowd, does not mean someone who is not as strong of a presenter has more anxiety than I do. Anxiety is not related to your personality; they are two separate entities and while one may be affected by the other at times, they are not always mutually inclusive.

* * *

The commonly used phrase "body image" refers directly to "the subjective picture or mental image of one's own body." Does this mean that the given definition is exclusively what body image is? Not necessarily, but it does mean it is more complex than originally suggested.

Body image is usually talked about in one of two ways: negative body image or positive body image. Negative body image encompasses those who are struggling, like my friend Brooke and myself, whereas positive body image usually describes the ideal outlook one aspires to have on body image.

In fact, fifty-eight percent of college-aged girls feel pressured to be a certain weight.[29]

Body image can get tricky, especially because the way one views their body is not always true to what their body actually looks like. It is important to remember that embracing your body the way that it is and treating it with respect and love will make you the healthiest you can be.

I like to think of my body as an expression of myself. I wear clothes that make me feel confident when I walk into a room. I eat foods that make me feel satisfied when I finish my meal. I express body language in a way that demonstrates how I want those around me to receive my presence.

By presenting my body as an expression that I am proud of, it makes it easier to embrace my body the way that it is and celebrate my body image for all of its imperfections.

---

29 National Association of Anorexia Nervosa and Associated Disorders. "Eating Disorders Statistics." ANAD. (2014).

* * *

Mental health is an often overused and misunderstood term. It is an overlooked topic that is classified as taboo by many facets of society. Simply defined it is "a person's condition with regard to their psychological and emotional well-being."[30]

Why then is it considered so taboo? People often feel uncomfortable addressing the psychological and emotional well-being of others because they are not stable in their own well-being. This results in the shaming of others for their psychological or emotional state. If we were to band together and support one another, we might be able to avoid the escalation of numerous insecurities that each and every one of us have. Why is it that we never question going to the doctor when we are physically sick, but we never consider going to the doctor when we are emotionally sick?

In terms of mental health, I think it is easy to fall into the trap of avoidance.

"Of the 450 million people worldwide who suffer from mental health conditions, the majority, being 60%, do not receive any form of care."[31]

---

30 Definition of mental health. *Dictionary.Com.* (2019).
31 Friedman, M. "The Stigma Of Mental Illness Is Making Us Sicker". *Psychology Today.* (2014).

We don't necessarily actively not talk about the topic, but rather we just gloss over it. I believe it is important to not feel shameful for struggling. I, myself, take medications for anxiety-triggered chronic migraines. I should not have to hide my situation because select facets of society feel it is taboo. Rather we should embrace our insecurities and maybe we can start to cope with them slowly through the power of support and empowerment.

Another misconception about mental health is that the journey is like climbing a mountain. You battle to the top and then cruise down the other side, looking back at all of the lessons you learned as you walk away from the struggles altogether. Anyone who has ever suffered from any type of mental health battle knows that's not true, whether mild or debilitating, the reality is much more complex. It is a journey of never-ending mountains, hills and foothills. The moment you feel like you are cruising down the other side of a mountain, a hill presents itself for you to have to battle yet again. While this may be very discouraging at times, I like to embrace the hills as reminders of how strong I am. The moments of 'cruising', better known as joy or bliss, become all the more rewarding when you overcame a battle to revel in them.

* * *

Lastly, the definition of the term survivor is definitely not all-encompassing of the many uses of the word. Plainly put, it is "a person who survives, especially a person remaining alive after an event in which others have died."[32]

This, however, does not even begin to address the countless survivors of many events that did not necessarily grapple with death. These events are usually quite traumatic for many other reasons, such as the events I spoke of previously, one of which being sexual assault.

Survivorship, in regards to sexual assault, means so much more than just being alive, rather you are living. Living with the lingering effects of trauma, living with the fear of a repeat offense, living with the uneasiness of trusting again, living through a constant struggle. You are also living with a resilience and strength unique to you. All survivorship of sexual assault does not look the same, however, for none of those survivors does it just simply mean to be alive.

* * *

These are all quite complex terms to make sense of. They do not necessarily have straightforward resources or a clear-cut path to understanding them.

---

32 Definition of survivor. *Dictionary.Com.* (2019).

Some resources I feel are of note are Rachel Hollis's *Girl, Wash Your Face* and *Girl, Stop Apologizing,* Aly Raisman's *Fierce,* Rachael Denhollander's *What is a Girl Worth?* and Brené Brown's *The Gifts of Imperfection: Let Go of Who You Think You're Supposed to Be and Embrace Who You Are.*

Hollis's books were blunt, but personal in an inviting way. She often addresses her readers directly, which is something I admired about her book and drew inspiration from for my own book.

Raisman's book was much more narrative, however, and it demonstrates clear strength and resilience throughout her experiences. She is candid with the reader in an endearing way.

Denhollander's book was thought-provoking, challenging you to think further about the Nassar case through the eyes of the survivors who lived it. She demonstrates strength and inspiration through her raw honesty.

Brown's book was a bit more technical, but struck a balance between research and personal experience that made the book less intimidating. It was refreshing to have a professional in the field sharing her intimate experiences with her readers.

* * *

Lastly, I would like to offer myself as a resource for any and all reasons. Feel free to email me at *spergola@umich.edu* at any time. Sometimes, all we need is a hand in our battle to truly feel like the warrior we are.

PART THREE

LOOKING FORWARD

CHAPTER 18

THERE IS LIFE BEYOND THE GYM'S FOUR WALLS

This was a fact that was definitely hard to swallow.

Life for nearly my first sixteen years, as I have detailed extensively throughout this book journey, revolved strictly around the gym. I wasn't really sure what I liked other than gymnastics. I had such a deep-rooted love and passion for gymnastics, I almost didn't have room inside of me for anything else. Now that there was this void to fill, I had no idea where to start in attempting to fill it. My senior year of high school was a weird mix of exploring cheerleading, school social settings, and clothes other than a leotard and relaxation. The only problem was, I hated relaxation, as this seemed to be synonymous with "bored."

The only thing that sort of stuck was my newfound enjoyment for clothing. I could express my mood of the day through the colors I wore and the style I encompassed. I really enjoyed the sense of agency I felt being able to choose what vibe I would emulate to the world each day. The only thing stopping me from really embracing this on a daily basis in high school was my school uniform. This didn't come to full fruition until later in college when I began to channel my creative side more wholly.

* * *

When it came to deciding what I would be studying in college, I decided this when I was still a gymnast. I was going to become a nurse since I already understood medicine fairly well having been to about a billion doctors over the years. This was also considered a job with growth that was stable and consistent. These were all things I was familiar and comfortable with. I was passionate about helping people and it was fulfilling to me to know I would be able to put that into practice in my everyday work.

Upon arriving to the University of Michigan's beautiful Ann Arbor campus, the first order of business was scoping out the gymnastics program. My parents and I entered the gymnastics practice facility. There were Big Ten trophies lining the walls with old photos of the past teams that had been awarded them. We glanced over them as we ventured toward the gym itself. I reached the doorway of the empty gym and completely uncontrollably and almost instantaneously, tears poured down my face. I stayed facing the open doorway, looking into a gym filled with equipment I would never get the chance to use. Big Ten Championship banners hung from the rafters and I would never get the chance to compete for one. I silently sobbed so my parents couldn't hear me.

Michigan's legendary coach, Bev Plocki, emerged from her office kindly greeting my parents. I heard them behind me, but I remained frozen staring blankly into the gym. My parents tapped my shoulder, appalled by my rude dismissal of Bev's presence, knowing my admiration of her extremely successful coaching career. As I turned slowly, wiping my face and attempting to gather myself, all three of their faces read surprise.

I uttered slowly taking a deep breath, "Hi. I'm so sorry. I don't know what's wrong with me right now." She smiled and I knew she understood our shared passion for this sport.

A calm came over me and the embarrassment faded away. We chatted for a bit and she shockingly offered me a position as the gymnastics team's manager. Unfortunately, as we spoke more, we realized my nursing major was too time-consuming to commit to this honorable position. I left the facility, defeated and again silent.

Sure enough, one year into college I had opted to change my major and found myself lost and empty all over again. I felt like I lost my identity again, struggling with my calling and not prioritizing myself and my mental health. Upon my mom's suggestion, I considered going back to pay Bev a visit to see if she would allow me to take on the manager position now that my new major would not be nearly as time-consuming. I thought back to my sobbing self in the doorway of the empty gym and instantly shied away from entering that facility again. I was embarrassed of my weakness at the time and terrified it would happen again, but this time in front of the gymnasts. Even worse, I was scared the gymnasts would think I was a failure and wannabe of sorts.

I found myself straying away from a sport I had so much love and passion for and feeling quite empty again.

* * *

This led me to pursue a path I had not expected. I joined SHEI Magazine, a student-run fashion magazine on campus. This was out of my comfort zone in many ways, but I thought it would be good to pursue something entirely new. I joined the social media team and I really enjoyed the content we were producing. It was inclusive, diverse, and celebratory.

Two years later, I got so involved and identified such commitment to the work that I was doing that I ran for and got elected the Publisher of SHEI, which heads the business department of the fashion magazine, for my senior year. The real value was learning how to immerse myself in uncharted territory and embrace every path that came along throughout the journey. This is something that allowed me to embrace my creativity and challenge my boundaries every day. Being Publisher instilled confidence in myself and my decisions, and independence in my thoughts and my actions. While my experience as Publisher was definitely challenging at times, it has been extremely rewarding both professionally and personally.

Not only was I growing professionally and personally through this experience, but I gained an invaluable friendship in the process. My co-leader in the organization, the Editor-in-Chief, Liv Velarde, is one of the most candid and supportive people I know. She empowered me through our positions at SHEI, supporting my every decision unwaveringly. She also empowered me through our friendship outside of SHEI, encouraging me to share my voice constantly. I am extremely grateful to have found her.

* * *

The 2018 Fall semester of my senior year, I took a class where the professor tended to tear the students down rather than build them up. We had an assignment that challenged us to "pitch" ourselves to our classmates to be a potential partner in a group project we would be doing. While most spoke about the various professional experiences they had, I chose to take a more personal route discussing my gymnastics career and sexual assault experiences briefly. This was untraditional and bold of me to do, especially in a classroom setting. I figured, however, that this would give the most candid demonstration of myself and my personality. As people stood before me presenting their own "pitch" I began to slump in my seat. I wondered what they would think of me and questioned whether I had taken the right approach to the project.

What ultimately came of it, however, was wonderful.

I stood, voice wavering slightly as I spoke. At first, I did not let my eyes venture off the paper I was reading from. Finally, halfway through, I glanced up into the crowd of students. Sure, there were some students not paying attention and likely browsing Facebook on their laptops, but those that were paying attention stared at me with inviting eyes.

I felt empowered and strong, something I did not expect to feel during this presentation. I stepped out of my comfort zone and while not everyone welcomed me with open arms, someone who eventually became very important to me, did. Liv Karas, a then member of the Michigan gymnastics team, approached me at the end of class. She was floored by my poise and strength and recognized my passion for the sport of gymnastics. I was flattered by her interest in me and thrilled for someone to have identified my passion, especially someone whom I shared that passion with.

* * *

Remember that fear that the gymnasts would think I was a failure? It was quite the opposite. Liv has allowed me to truly immerse myself in the gymnastics world again. Through attending some mock competitions in their practice gym (that I was dreading reentering beforehand) and cheering her on vehemently from the seats in Crisler arena during all of their home meets, I have fallen back in love with the sport of gymnastics. Away meets are spent with my eyes glued to my computer live streaming the content while I still cheer vehemently as if I was in the arena with her.

She has been extra special to me, making me feel as though I can still embrace my love and passion for the sport of gymnastics even though it is through the other side of the glass now. These different outlets that I now engage with are just as rewarding and have made me feel at home once again in a gymnastics gym.

Our friendship, however, goes much deeper than just gymnastics. Liv is a warrior in so many ways, one being suffering extreme injury and fighting her way back to success. Her unwavering optimism and genuine spirit have allowed me to find a very special friend in her that I value greatly.

This marriage of lifelong passion for gymnastics and new-found passion in other facets of life has allowed me to flourish both professionally and personally.

* * *

Reentering that practice facility once again, being faced with the same place that had provided me a deep-flowing sense of loss, was extremely difficult. I had second guessed going numerous times and had an internal fight standing outside the door before entering. Taking that step through the door opened a world of possibilities for me.

It proved that I could leave the past behind and reenter this world in a new way. It also proved that the sport of gymnastics is not what failed me, rather the culture of gymnastics is what drove me to dark places. Lastly, it proved that I could once again fall in love with this sport and I didn't have to be a gymnast to do so.

I could, in fact, conquer the challenges that came with the negatives I had experienced. I am not what happened to me, I am what I choose to become. And most of all, I could follow my calling and encompass fulfillment in my life.

CHAPTER 19

A LETTER FROM MY MOM: *OPEN YOUR HEARTS...* *AND YOUR EARS*

———

As a mom of a competitive gymnast, as well as a sexual assault survivor, my message to parents is simple, LISTEN to your children.

Looking back on my relationship with my amazing daughter, Serena, I wish I would have done a few things differently. Then, maybe I wouldn't constantly be asking myself "what if?"

* * *

Serena began her gymnastics career at the ripe age of four years old. Her level of passion, commitment, and desire for the sport was truly incredible. I admired, and still admire, her for it. But what if, I was a better mentor to her first gymnastics coach? While I believe she really cared for the athletes she was training, she could have been taught a better approach in certain situations that could have maybe, just maybe, changed her coaching style to a more positive one. What if I didn't allow the coaches training Serena in seventh and eighth grade to push her so hard when her body was not mature enough to handle the impact which led to the fractures in her back? What if I empowered my daughter to do the right thing for herself before focusing on others first? What if I didn't push her so hard to train at a level that her body couldn't handle? Maybe, just maybe, things would have been different. Maybe she would not have been assaulted by her boyfriend. Or drugged by a date. Or I can't even imagine, nor do I want to imagine, what would have happened when the boy burst into the bathroom if another person did not enter the room.

And thus, I struggle with these things on a daily basis.

* * *

While my relationship with Serena has always been incredible, I believe I did her a disservice as a young girl. This led to her being in relationships and surrounding herself with people who were truly not her *friends*, did not have her back, and were not morally good people. I will live with that guilt for the rest of my life and I believe I deserve that. I know I need to forgive myself, but as a mom you NEVER want your child to experience a hangnail, let alone the horrible things my daughter experienced.

And thus, I struggle with these things on a daily basis.

* * *

On a more positive note, I am in awe of how she has truly embraced everything that has happened to her. Through years of therapy, she has identified her silver lining and her therapist is a person who I am beyond thankful for. She helped Serena to share these horrible events with me, as well as, helped her to understand that she is a survivor, not a victim. This has empowered her to write this book and share her story with the world, with the hope that maybe she could help just one person identify their silver lining. The title truly is so appropriate.

Serena has fallen back in love with the sport of gymnastics, which I am so grateful for. At its very core, gymnastics is an incredible sport and what it gives to young athletes is beyond words. Gymnasts are very special people. I always say it is the only sport you strive for perfection that will likely never be obtained, but will always be the goal. Well, maybe in college, perfection can sometimes be achieved, if you are lucky enough to have the opportunity to be a college gymnast in the first place. The confidence, perseverance, persistence, focus, commitment, grace, strength, independence, and determination, to just name a few, this sport gives your child is invaluable and I am thankful that although Serena did not achieve at the level she hoped to due to injury, this sport has given her far beyond the skills taught in four walls of a gymnastics facility. This sport has also given Serena her forever friends, friends she knows will always have her back and are there for her always. These young ladies are my gymnastics children and I love them like my own and I am truly thankful for their friendship with Serena.

* * *

Today, my relationship with Serena couldn't be stronger.

She is my hero; I admire her strength, respect her opinion, and believe in her at the very soul. She is truly my best friend. And I know to some that may sound weird, but Serena is an adult now and we share things on an adult level. I LISTEN to her, truly LISTEN. She is beyond intelligent. The people's lives that she enters see the light she exudes. To watch this when she meets someone for the first time is heartwarming.

You would never know the darkness she has been through; you would assume that she has it all and has never had a difficult moment in her life. She has now graduated from the University of Michigan, is renting a luxury apartment in the Big Apple, and has begun her career in advertising. I know success in her career is at her fingertips. Finally, she has written this incredible book and has shared with the entire world every part of her from her darkest moments to her greatest successes. This is admirable to want to share and I believe it will resonate with an insurmountable amount of people.

I have to remind myself that she is just twenty-one years of age, she is an old soul, her maturity is a blessing, and I am a proud momma!

* * *

As far as USA Gymnastics goes, I believe they need to do a better job training their members, not just through online courses or the yearly Regional and National Congress that they host. I believe there should be mandatory in-person training for anyone who wants to be a gymnastics coach. There should be written and hands-on testing to make sure coaches understand how to correctly coach athletes, mentally, physically, and emotionally. There should also be mandatory continued education courses. It should be the responsibility of the coaches to pay for, as well as attend these classes and they should be tested at the close to be sure they fully understand everything they were taught.

Case in point, USA Gymnastics made it mandatory for its members to take the Safe Sport Course. While I believe this is absolutely necessary, it should absolutely not be online. It should be a class that requires in-person participation by all members, as well as testing. The culture of this sport needs to change and the only way to do so is to treat this wonderful sport with the respect it deserves.

* * *

Today, I am part owner of a gymnastics facility and I am proud to say that the culture in my gym is extremely positive. The athletes' well-being is our top priority, mentally, emotionally, and physically. We are a family and we understand gymnastics reaches far beyond the four walls of the gym. I know the level of commitment, focus, strength, flexibility, and dedication, to name a few, required to achieve in this sport. But, what I also know now and would never allow, is abuse on any level. What you say and how you say it impacts these young athletes, not just today, but for the rest of their lives.

Words are powerful and they mold how a child sees themselves, so our approach is always positive. This doesn't mean athletes never get frustrated and there are no tears, but the tears are not from being made to feel less than anyone else by any one of our coaches. This culture is starting to catch on, even though there are still parents who I like to say are "still drinking the Kool Aid" and believe that yelling is the only way to bring about success.

It's unfortunate, but it's a fact.

* * *

I leave you now with these final thoughts: Talk to your children; even when they don't want to, even when you don't want to.

Listen to your children; even if there are a lot of things going on in your life and even when you do not agree with their thoughts, respect them.

Discuss their lives, not just gymnastics, or their sport of choice, but rather help them to understand how incredible they are.

Remember you created this wonderful human. Your children are a gift and it's your job to help them become strong, confident adults. Take this job seriously; it is the most important and most rewarding job you have. Trust me, you will make mistakes; admit to them and move on. You will do better next time as mistakes teach us lessons. My hope for anyone reading this is that you will take my words seriously and do a better job than I did.

That being said, I am very lucky to have such a strong, confident woman who sees past my flaws and makes me feel like an amazing mom every day!

CHAPTER 20

HEY USA GYMNASTICS, PLEASE KINDLY DO YOUR PART!

I have lightly danced around this topic thus far, however, I do not feel that is enough. While I love the sport of gymnastics, more needs to be done by USA Gymnastics. They're enabling the problem and it continues to grow because of them.

Previously, I mentioned how I don't feel the sport itself is the problem, rather it is the culture surrounding the sport. I touched on a few of the factors adding to this culture already, such as the promotion of emotionlessness and the emphasis on an ideal body type. The one factor I haven't fully tackled, and quite similarly USA Gymnastics hasn't fully tackled, is the overhaul of all policies, or lack thereof, that enabled the Larry Nassar events.

It is hard to ensure the complete and total safety of athletes, specifically gymnasts in this case, if the same policies that enabled such a horrifying event are still a part of the ruling organization of the sport. More so, it is hard to believe the organization is truly trying to promote positive change for the future when they have not taken full responsibility for their actions and involvement in the Nassar events. Rather, they blame individuals where systemic accountability is essential. Not only are the policies that are in place not successful in protecting athletes from all forms of abuse, there are not enough policies in place to ensure that athletes will be trusted and protected in the future.

* * *

Deborah Daniels, the Managing Partner of Indianapolis-based Krieg DeVault LLP and a former federal prosecutor, conducted an independent review of USA Gymnastics' bylaws, policies, procedures, and practices related to handling sexual misconduct matters. In such review she made various recommendations, some of which being:

- Require immediate reporting of suspected abuse.

- Create a clear protocol for response to abuse complaints.

- Permit third-party reporting.

- Remove the president from a "controlling role" in handling complaints.

- Strengthen the Safe Sport Policy and require it to be adopted in full by member clubs.

- Develop a disciplinary process for clubs found to be in violation of the Safe Sport Policy.

- Consider requiring certification for coaches before they're hired by member clubs.

- Create and require annual training in abuse policies, procedures, and reporting mechanisms.

- Educate parents and athletes on abuse prevention on an annual basis.

- Hire a Safe Sport director. (The U.S. Center for SafeSport is an independent nonprofit committed to ending all forms of abuse in sport. This includes bullying, harassment, hazing, physical abuse, emotional abuse, and sexual misconduct and abuse. The Center is the first and only national organization of its kind. The Center provides services to sport entities on abuse prevention techniques, policies, and programs and provides a safe, professional, and confidential place for individuals to report sexual abuse within the U.S. Olympic and Paralympic Movements.[33])[34]

* * *

While it remains unknown whether Daniels's law firm was involved in covering up the Nassar reporting as they were happening, the above recommendations are very necessary for USA Gymnastics to become a more reliable and trustworthy organization that is athlete centric and allows the athletes to feel safe and protected.

Additionally, programs such as Aly Raisman's Darkness to Light are also of great importance for both athletes and coaches. "Darkness to Light is a non-profit committed to empowering adults to prevent child sexual abuse. Our work is guided by the vision of a world free from child sexual abuse,

---

33 "Who We Are." *Safesport*. (2019).

34 Daniels, J.D., Deborah J. "Report to USA Gymnastics on Proposed Policy and Procedural Changes for the Protection of Young Athletes." Krieg DeVault with assistance from Praesidium. (2017).

where children can grow up happy, healthy and safe. We know that prevention is possible, and we believe that it is an adult responsibility to protect children. We exist to empower people to prevent child sexual abuse. Children deserve to grow up happy and healthy, with their sexual boundaries intact. Education is the first step."[35] This program is free of charge with Aly's promo code "fliptheswitch," which makes it all the more frustrating that more people are not fully educated on the topic. The training should not stop here. There should be a schooling, both written and hands-on, for all coaches to attend.

Some might argue that there is Regional and National Congress offered for hands-on, in-person training. Regional Congress provides education to instructors, coaches, judges, and gymnastics business owners in each region. Education and training enable everyone to effectively and professionally serve in the development of young gymnasts across the country.[36] National Congress provides a valuable opportunity for gymnastics professionals around the country to attend educational presentations, as well as a number of live demonstrations, on a variety of topics, including coaching, judging, business, preschool, school-age/recreational, sports

35 "About Darkness to Light - Darkness to Light." *Darkness to Light.* (2019).
36 "USA Gymnastics Regional Congress." *USA Gymnastics Regional Congress.* (2019).

science, fitness, safe sport and more.[37] Regional and National Congress are not mandatory and are, therefore, not enough to further the education of the coaches as those who elect to attend most likely already take measures to further their education, whereas those who elect not to attend most likely do not take these measures.

The continuing education should be mandatory and the responsibility of the coaches to cover the cost and complete. If the coaches are truly dedicated to their athletes, then they should have no qualms making this continuing education their responsibility as it enforces that the gymnasts are their priority.

* * *

All forms of abuse MUST stop and the first steps in this becoming a reality are awareness and education.

---

37 "About Congress | USA Gymnastics National Congress." *USA Gymnastics National Congress.* (2019).

CHAPTER 21

LOVE YOURSELF AND THE OTHERS WILL FOLLOW

———

Disclaimer: I am very well aware of how cliché loving yourself sounds.

The thing is, the oversaturated media version of loving yourself and the true, raw, honest version of loving yourself are quite different. While the media version may be more glamorous, and don't get me wrong, a glass of wine in a bubble bath with a face mask on reading a good book right after you just made a very satisfying Lululemon purchase definitely can be fulfilling as well, the true version of loving yourself allows for a lifetime of fulfillment, rather than just one night, or sometimes just one hour.

* * *

Loving yourself starts with, and really culminates with, your values.

Identifying them, figuring out how they look in the real world beyond some nuanced, conceptual version of them, and then encompassing them in your everyday life. This means you need to keep those values at the forefront of your mind at all times, both professionally and personally.

* * *

When you meet someone, think about how their values compare to your values. Do they align with them? Or, do they contradict them? Do they compliment your own? Or, are theirs detrimental to your own? This means I surround myself with my incredibly supportive and inspirational parents, my very loving family and my spontaneous friends (Y'all know who you are).

* * *

When you are looking for a job, think about how it fits into your values. Does their workplace culture align with your values? Or, does it contradict them? Does their social impact align with your own? Does it compliment your own? Or, is it detrimental to your own? This means you won't take every offer you get. And trust me, being a freshly minted alumni, I know how scary that sounds. Job hunting is overwhelming as is, add in vehemently ensuring it aligns with your values and it becomes a dark maze.

This also doesn't mean you won't take some jobs that you later realize don't align with your values. That is totally okay too, as a matter of fact it is normal. The most important thing is focusing on immersing yourself in an environment that brings you up, not tears you down. Prioritize what fuels the passion inside of you and makes you look forward to work the next day. Recognize what gets you out of bed in the morning and then pursue that in the professional world. Work doesn't have to feel like work when you are doing what you love.

* * *

Another essential aspect of loving myself was identifying, and truly believing that I am not the problem. This has been a really hard concept for me to wrap my head around. While I have attempted to make sense of it for years now, writing this book has truly brought this belief to the forefront. Writing my experiences down on paper has allowed me to remove myself from the equation and hear the story as if it was someone else's. Sometimes, when things hit too close to home, they are hard to paint a clear picture of.

I can now say, with full confidence, I am not the problem. And I never was.

* * *

Once I discovered my values, and decided to prioritize them even in the hardest areas of my life, I was able to truly and fully love myself. This allows me to show up for my friends and family in a way I was not able to before. It allows me to immerse myself in my passions and to set goals that I'm confident I can reach. It allows me to aspire to things that seem so much bigger and greater than myself, and have faith that they will one day happen.

Life requires risk, but risk means unsafe territory and vulnerability. By grounding myself in my values, I have been able to maintain security in the uncharted territory that I continue to explore.

And most of all, I have been able to identify and embrace my silver lining.

CHAPTER 22

IN A WORLD WHERE YOU CAN BE ANYTHING, BE KIND

———

So, what does my silver lining look like today? It's all about the little wins in the larger battle we call life.

* * *

There was a time when I thought I would never be able to walk down the street alone, never mind the thought of living alone. I now live in an apartment in Manhattan alone... and I love it.

There was a time when I thought I would never be able to talk in front of a crowd without developing a migraine and hyperventilating for hours, sometimes days beforehand. I now have presented in front of crowds of 150+ and smiled while I did it... and actually looked forward to doing it beforehand.

There was a time when I couldn't go one day without having an anxiety attack, let alone a whole five months. I am now able to control my emotions and make sense of what I am feeling... all without having a breakdown.

* * *

My life has been and continues to be far from perfect.

There will always be new challenges to face and new obstacles to overcome, but when you are grounded in optimism and empowerment you are ready to take on anything the world throws your way. Remembering that there is no battle I cannot fight is essential to fighting the next battle that comes my way. Remember, "We are all warriors fighting to be our best selves every day." My life looks very regular from the outside looking in. Without reading this book, many would not know I have faced many of the experiences I have.

That's the thing—we all have a story.

Share yours. Not with just anyone, but with those who are worth sharing it with. Be vulnerable, but with those who deserve to experience your vulnerabilities. To this day I don't love talking about those traumatizing experiences, but when I do let people into that part of my life, I feel so much stronger. Sharing your story can help others, whether it be helping them to deal with a situation in their life or helping them to better understand you, all of it is helpful.

My friend, Liv Velarde, wrote an article for a feminist magazine at the University of Michigan called *What the F*. She wrote this one paragraph that was so simple, but it has stuck with me even months after reading it. "We seek comfort and healing in various ways, but our motto is that only survivors know what is best for them in their individual cases. This makes sense; no one should tell another person the right or wrong way to deal with trauma. But I've always had this suspicion that we parrot this line not because we believe in the inner compass of every individual survivor, but because none of us has ever found a satisfying answer. Telling survivors to search within themselves and find their personalized solutions is easier than admitting that there isn't a straightforward path to healing."[38]

With that in mind, I challenge you to accept this long winding road to healing in its entirety; the bumps, the dark spots, the light patches, and even the detours. I challenge you to

---

38   Velarde, O. "The Worry Stone." *What The F Magazine.* (2018).

believe that though there may not be a perfect solution, there is your solution. You don't have to erase your past to move onto your future. As a matter of fact, embracing your past in all that it taught you and how it strengthened you for the future will be much more satisfying.

And most of all, I urge you to confidently believe in your heart of hearts, that you are not the problem. Because I guarantee you, you are not.

* * *

For all of my fellow planners out there, I empathize with you. I realize how painstakingly hard it is to accept that life does not follow a straightforward path.

I am the true definition of the ultimate planner. Trust me, my mom and my friends would most definitely agree. I spend countless hours of every day planning out the day, the week, the month, the year, the next 2 years, the next 5 years, the next 10 years, the next 20 years... you get the point. I have a plan for when I will buy a house, when I will get married, when I will have children, when I will eat breakfast, when I will finish my coffee and start hydrating with water for the day... you name the event, big or small, and I have a time, day, location and attendee list for it all planned out perfectly in my head. Not only that, but I also have a back-up plan, a plan B if you will. This is a re-worked plan for when my first plan inevitably does not play out how I had planned for it to.

Has anything ever followed my plan? Not once. If you can't tell by this point, my life has strayed far from my plan. Nothing I wrote about in this book was something I planned for. Nothing I wrote about in this book was something I re-planned for after my first plan got messed up. Frankly, nothing in this book is something anyone would plan for. Nonetheless, this is the life I have been meant to live. I have to have faith in my path, even when my path does not make any sense in the present moment.

This doesn't mean I won't still sit with my planner and erase and re-work my daily, weekly, monthly and yearly plans incessantly. But what it does mean is that when my plan does not follow its A route, B route, C route or even D route, I will persist on and have faith in the E route. Because after all, the E route has brought me to where I am today and I know in my heart that I am meant to be here finishing my book-writing journey and soaking in all of the lessons it has taught me. Finally, I know I am meant to be here sharing those lessons with you in the hopes that they will empower you like they have empowered me.

* * *

We are faced with many choices each and every day. Choose to be kind.

You will meet many people that choose to be horribly mean, or others that choose to be really nice to your face, but are betraying you behind your back, and also others who choose to be kind. Surround yourself with those who make that same choice as you—to be kind. After all, just like the shirt my friend's mom bought me for my birthday says, "In a world where you can be anything, be kind."

THE FREEING FEELING OF EMPOWERMENT

———

Thank you for sharing in this storytelling journey with me.

I have enjoyed the journey of exploring this story through a lens I have not yet shared publicly. Further reflection, both internally and externally, has allowed me to better understand my feelings. Something I have noticed about myself throughout this journey is that the things that have caused me the most pain are also the things I avoid talking about. Finally coming to talk about these things has helped me to make more sense of why I felt the way I did and how I can learn from those past experiences and use them to my benefit in the future.

Today, I spend most of my time focusing on happiness.

There are days where this feels impossible. It feels as though the entire world in against me and there is absolutely nothing to be happy about. That is not only okay, but it is normal. I find it to be important to prioritize those things that make me the happiest and immerse myself in those. I also explore why other things do not bring me happiness. If I can rid myself of these things, I do. That's not to say that is always an easy feat. Sometimes, the negative thing is someone whom I consider a friend, other times it is a family situation that is bogging me down. Oftentimes it's a simple, everyday nuisance that I can easily remove from my life. Unfortunately, we can't avoid all negative, but what we can do is try to extract the positive from the negative.

Commonplace within my life has been this recurring feeling of self-doubt and worthlessness. The toying back and forth with the idea that I can handle the obstacle life presents me with. Sure, sometimes, the obstacle is simple and I come out on the other side successful and pleased with the result almost naturally. There are other times where overcoming the obstacle is not as straightforward; where I need to employ true belief in myself to successfully overcome it.

Then there are the times that I don't have full control over the situation at hand; when I have to rely on the good of others and the good of the world to have things fall into place the way I want them to. Those are the real challenges in life for me; trusting in others. Life doesn't follow an exact formula, rather it surprises us. Be mindful of who you trust, but don't close yourself off completely to those who have been tried and true just because you are scared of being vulnerable.

There is almost always a positive that comes from a negative situation, such as resilience and strength. Trust in yourself and your instincts. Make the hard choices in life because those are the most rewarding. Choose your happiness and your passions, even when it feels like that is impossible to do. And always remember, you are not the problem.

* * *

To the young gymnasts-

Trust your gut.

I cannot tell you how many times my gut told me something seemed off, but I questioned myself and wouldn't listen to it. You know yourself better than anyone else. When you are in pain, listen to your body no matter how badly you want to continue practice. One day of rest is better than three months of injury (if you listen to me about nothing else, please listen to me on this). Remember you are so much more than just a gymnast. You are a beautiful, talented person who has mastered a sport very few can, but that doesn't mean you can't have a life beyond those four walls. Engage in other interests, or even other activities. An interest or activity can become a career down the line, but unfortunately gymnastics cannot. Very few people will become Olympians and no matter how badly we wish and hope and work for this to be us, unexpected things happen that we never see coming (again, trust me on this). Lastly, enjoy your time in the gym. The beauty of the sport of gymnastics is that we often develop a deep-flowing passion for the sport as a result of the commitment and challenges we endured.

Bask in the beauty of being a gymnast, it absolutely is the very best sport.

To the fellow former gymnasts-

Don't fall out of love with the sport.

It brought us so many wonderful things, sometimes it's okay to overlook the negative ones. Be conscious of the bad habits it instilled in us, but don't let them run your life. Embrace your emotions, no matter how scary they seem or how vulnerable they make you feel. It is good to feel things, the sad, the happy, and everything in between. Don't let anything or anyone manipulate you into doing something you don't want to do. You are in control of you, always remember that. Last, but definitely not least, be proud that you were a gymnast.

Enjoy the fact that we performed one of, arguably, the most difficult sports in the world and know that you can take on any challenge life throws at you.

To the parents of gymnasts-

Trust your children.

When they are in pain, listen to them. When they feel uncomfortable, listen to them. When they feel overworked, listen to them. But most of all, listen to your parental instincts because they are rarely wrong. While nothing that happened to me is my mom's fault in any way, shape, or form, I know for a fact she wishes she would have listened to her parental instincts more often early on when the intensity of the sport picked up steam. No matter how talented your children are, don't push them too hard. They will eventually burn out and resent either you or themselves, neither of these are good results.

Most of all, remind them they are more than just a gymnast. Remind them just how beautiful and talented and capable and worthy they are. Empower them to pursue their best selves.

* * *

You got this.

Life is about finding your silver lining and embracing it.

xoxo- Serena

APPENDIX

INTRODUCTION

Definition of silver lining. *Merriam-Webster.Com.* (2019).

Ekern, J. "Risks of Eating Disorders for Athletes & Successful Recovery." *Eating Disorder Hope.* (2011).

Evans, T. "Child Advocate, Former Prosecutor Join USA Gymnastics in Move to Better Protect Athletes." *Indystar.Com.* (2017).

Evans, T., Alesia, M. and Kwiatkowski, M. "Indystar's Investigation on Sexual Abuse in Gymnastics: What We Know." *Indystar.Com.* (2016).

Westermann, R., Giblin, M., Vaske, A., Grosso, K. and Wolf, B. *Evaluation of Men's and Women's Gymnastics Injuries.* National Center for Biotechnology Information. (2015).

CHAPTER 1

"BBC News | EUROPE | Romanian Gymnasts Faked Age to Compete.". *News. Bbc.Co.Uk.* (2002)

Catching up with Jordyn Wieber and Kamerin Moore." USA Gymnastics. (2008).

Phillips, I. "A Gymnastics Coach Explains Why Female Gymnasts Are So Young." INSIDER. (2016).

Raisman, A. Fierce: How Competing for Myself Changed Everything. Little, Brown Books for Young Readers. (2018).

Reed, B. "Aly Raisman On the Importance of the Team Competition." *Flogymnastics.Com.* (2015).

CHAPTER 4

Corbett, S. "Olympic Gymnast Aly Raisman's Memoir Holds Painful Revelations". *Publishersweekly.Com.* (2017).

"Gymnastics." *Teamusa.Org.* (2019).

CHAPTER 5

"Benefits of Gymnastics." Champaign Gymnastics Academy. (2019).

"Benefits of Gymnastics." Springfit. (2019).

Burgdorf, T. "Benefits of Gymnastics." Gymnastics Unlimited. (2019).

Mazzo, L. "Aly Raisman On What It's Like to Compete in a Sport That's All About Perfection." Shape. (2019).

Peszek, S. Instagram Post. (2019).

Schultz, J., O'Reilly, J. and Cahn, S.K. Women and Sports in the United States. Boston: Northeastern University Press. (2007).

Sharp, K. "Competitive Gymnastics for Young Girls: What to Expect." Howtheyplay. (2019).

"The Touchy Topic of Gymnasts and Body Weight, Eating Disorders and Nutrition (Part 1 of 4)." *Flogymnastics.Com.* (2014).

"Thoughts on Aly Raisman's Autobiography, 'Fierce.'" Teenage Struggles. (2018).

CHAPTER 8

Lao Tzu.

CHAPTER 12

"Could Yoga Hold the Key to Healing a Patient's Trauma?" NICABM. (2019).

CHAPTER 14

Kimble, C. and Chettiar, I.M. "Sexual Assault Remains Dramatically Under-Reported | Brennan Center for Justice." *Brennancenter.Org.* (2018).

Ladd, J. "The Reporting System That Sexual Assault Survivors Want." Presentation, TED. (2016).

"The Criminal Justice System: Statistics | RAINN." *Rainn.Org.* (2019).

CHAPTER 17

Definition of anxiety. *Dictionary.Com.* (2019).

Definition of mental health. *Dictionary.Com.* (2019).

Definition of survivor. *Dictionary.Com.* (2019).

Friedman, M. "The Stigma of Mental Illness Is Making Us Sicker." Psychology Today. (2014).

National Association of Anorexia Nervosa and Associated Disorders. "Eating Disorders Statistics." ANAD. (2014).

CHAPTER 19

"About Congress | USA Gymnastics National Congress." USA Gymnastics National Congress. (2019).

"About Darkness to Light - Darkness to Light.", Darkness to Light. (2019).

Daniels J.D., Deborah J. "Report to USA Gymnastics on Proposed Policy and Procedural Changes for the Protection of Young Athletes." Krieg DeVault with assistance from Praesidium. (2017).

"USA Gymnastics Regional Congress." USA Gymnastics Regional Congress. (2019).

"Who We Are." Safesport. (2019).

CHAPTER 21

Velarde, O. "The Worry Stone." *What the F Magazine.* (2018).

ACKNOWLEDGEMENTS

———

As I sit here writing the Acknowledgements section, I am overwhelmed with feelings of gratitude. The amount of support I have received throughout the process of publishing this book has been extremely humbling and entirely empowering. I can never truly express in words how very thankful I am for each and every person who has been a part of this book-writing journey thus far. So to all of you have contributed... from the bottom of my heart, thank you. This list of names is a true testament to the immense amount of love I have in my life.

As I wrote the final words to this book, I exhaled. I realize I have been holding my breath for years, worried about what others would think of me, worried about what others would say about me, but most importantly, worried what others would say *to* me. I now know that it is not my responsibility to protect everyone's feelings. I know that after reading this some people will not say all of the right things, and that is okay. Not everyone needs to see the world in the way that I do, but I also don't have to let those people discourage me from embracing my beliefs. I also know that those who have hurt me throughout the years need to own their actions, and hopefully make a decision to be a better human moving forward. Most of all, I know that there is still a part of me that fears these men that wronged me, but ultimately I have come to confidently believe I am not the problem and that I can no longer give in to that fear. I told them no, I told them to stop, and they made the decision to take advantage of me. That is a decision they need to own and live with, just like I have to own and live with the trauma that has resulted from that very decision that they made. I know that publishing this book will most likely be the most vulnerable thing I do in my lifetime and all I can hope for is that one individual feels empowered by it to take back their life and know that they are not the problem either.

A special thank you to the following people in the editing stages of my manuscript:

My Developmental Editor, Davida Smith-Keita, who challenged me to further my introspection and fully express my story.

My Marketing Editor, Barbara Hightower, may she Rest in Peace and be remembered as the kindhearted and pleasant soul that she was.

My dear friend and editor, Olivia Velarde, who invited me to candidly share my voice.

Eric Koester, Founder of Creator Institute, for introducing me to this program and encouraging me to take the leap and go on this journey.

And Brian Bies, Head of Publishing at New Degree Press, who laid the groundwork that made this book possible and guided me through every step of the process... we have finally arrived at a final product I am proud to call my book.

With all of that being said, thank you to everyone who gave me their time for a personal interview, pre-ordered the eBook, paperback, and multiple copies to make publishing possible, helped spread the word about *The Silver Lining* to gather amazing momentum, and helped me publish a book I am proud of. I am sincerely grateful for all of your help and support.

Melissa Grippa   Alana and Joe Maltese*

Lisa Pergola*   The Domill Family

The Boni Family

The Grimaldi Family*

Christina Maltese

Jennifer Webb

Lanette Lucksavage

The Sack Family*

AJ D'Ambrosio

Jessica Fallis

Dawn Minuto

Susan Fishelberg

Meghan Bonomi

Penny Stein

Eric Koester

Patricia Takeda and Ken Rhodes

Apoorvee Singhal

Kim Rhatigan*

Taryn Matthews

Joanne Coscino

Jacqueline Maddie

Danielle Messineo*

Alexa Pepe

The Hulser Family

Amanda Trau

Ilyssa Rosken

Jennifer Arena

Follett Carter

Zachary Rhodes

Lauren Farley

Ben Lambert*

Billy Paymaster

Christine Heck

Jeremy Masseth

Erin Malone

Robert Helstrom

Danielle Romano

Ralph Mack*

Sukatu Shah

The Grossman Family*

Michael Bonomo

Kristlyn Lyons

Robert Harteveldt

Christopher Howard

Beanie Zollweg

Theresa Palermo

Brooke Sender~

Louise Pasquale

Bonnie Klugman

Kathie Kelly

Laura Sommer

Elizabeth Shevins

Jessica Jackowicz

Karim Ibrahim

Robert Oringer*

Lauren Lucksavage

Ben Anderson

Thomas Pergola*

Lucy Pergola

Eric Raphael

Adam Katz*

Raquel Laneri

The Hayes Family

Neil Caracciolo

Marcus Collins*

Joe Pergola

Olivia Velarde

Diane Morrell*

Farmingdale
Gymnastics Academy*

Jennifer Russo*

Christopher Rhodes

Chris Milas

Raymond Walther

Kathy Gray

Marissa Rubinfeld

Stacia Mahoney

Donagene Jones

Lyn Wan*

The Alper Family*

Angela Jones

Jamie Simon

Robin Harper

Lauren Bifano

The McCann Family   Nicole Minuto

The Muhlbach Family

Key:
*multiple copies/campaign contributions
~featured interviewee